Size and Efficiency in Farming

D.K. BRITTON
Professor of Agricultural Economics
BERKELEY HILL
Lecturer in Agricultural Economics

Wye College
University of London

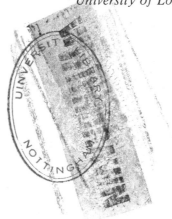

SAXON HOUSE | LEXINGTON BOOKS

Published by

SAXON HOUSE, Teakfield Limited,
Westmead, Farnborough, Hants., England

Reprinted 1979

ISBN 0 347 01043 1

Printed in Great Britain by
Ilfadrove Limited, Barry, Glamorgan, S.Wales

Contents

List of figures

List of tables

Acknowledgements

Thanks are due to the Ministry of Agriculture, Fisheries and Food (Agricultural Censuses and Surveys Branch) for assistance given in the provision of Farm Management Survey data on magnetic tape; and to Paul Kentish of the Statistical and Computing Unit of Wye College, University of London, for his patient and skilled work in computer programming which overcame the problems of incompatibility between the computer systems used by MAFF and Wye College and which resulted in numerous tables which he and Eric Maddison (formerly Head of the Statistical Unit at Wye College) kindly provided at our request.

1 Introduction

Whenever the current difficulties and the future prospects of agriculture are under discussion, it is not long before the question of the most desirable size of farm is raised. The relative merits of small and large farms have been argued for more than a century, and the issue is as lively now as it was in 1904 when Hermann Levy wrote that 'the question as to the best unit of agricultural management has been of increasing importance in England for the last twenty years'.[1] This question is closely intertwined with the problem of low incomes in agriculture. If small farms generally provide their occupiers with inadequate incomes, is this simply because they are small, or is it partly because they are not efficiently managed? This book attempts to throw light on the nature and extent of the relationship between size and efficiency, and to consider some of its implications for farmers and policy-makers.

The title of the book should not be taken to indicate that we have an uncritical obsession with size for its own sake (subscribing to the philosophy of 'the bigger, the better'), nor that we believe that efficiency (which we shall try to define and measure) should necessarily be the farmer's most important objective. We are convinced that William Cowper's observation that 'variety's the very spice of life' applies as much to agriculture as to other activities, and that a wide range of farm sizes will always co-exist, occupied by farmers with an equally wide variety of objectives, among which efficiency may not always be very high on the list.

Nevertheless, we do believe that the present British agricultural pattern of resource allocation between farms of different sizes is not necessarily the best that could be made, either in the interests of the farmers themselves or from the national point of view. The pattern itself is changing year by year towards having fewer but larger farms. In many ways such a change is to be welcomed. It is well known that farms which are small in acreage or small in terms of production tend to yield low incomes, and this being so, any movement which reduces the number of small farms and leaves the remaining farmers with larger businesses is likely to benefit the economic well-being of the agricultural population. However, even this apparently straightforward proposition does not take

1

into account the consequences for those farmers (and their families) who are displaced in the process of farm enlargement; neither does it answer the broader question of whether the economic well-being of farm families, inevitably measured in terms of the money payments which flow to and from them in the course of their farming activities, is the only or the ultimate criterion of what is the best among alternative patterns. We certainly do not rule out the possibility that a re-structuring of farm sizes which would result in a more prosperous agricultural community might nevertheless be accompanied by other less desirable features, such as a neglect of long-term considerations of good husbandry,[2] an increase in the strains and stresses experienced by farmers in their decision-making, a deterioration in the personal relationships between employer and employed, a disintegration of rural communities or a less attractive appearance of the countryside. Most economic and social changes bring about a new net balance of advantage and disadvantage, both within the situation of individual families and in the relations between them and the rest of the community; and a change in the structure of agriculture is undoubtedly no exception in being diverse in its effects.

Not surprisingly, therefore, we make no categorical statements pronouncing that all farms or farming operations of less than a certain size ought to disappear. Different people will make different judgements of what action, if any, is desirable 'in the national interest' or in the interest of anyone else, on the basis of the available evidence. We shall endeavour to assemble some of that evidence and to explore some of the interrelationships which underlie it.

This is not pioneering work. For many generations, agriculturists, agricultural historians and agricultural economists have pondered the question: what is the best size for a farm? Even if we insist that this question is misconceived because there is no identifiable optimum applicable to all farmers and all kinds of land and environmental conditions at any time, let alone over a period of rapid technological and social change, we have to acknowledge that, in many countries, a large number of studies have addressed themselves to this problem.[3]

Among the previous studies in this field, special mention must be made of the report on *Scale of Enterprise in Farming.* This report was published by H.M. Stationery Office in 1961 on behalf of the now defunct Office of the Minister for Science. It was prepared by the Natural Resources (Technical) Committee under the chairmanship of Sir Solly Zuckerman, and we shall refer to it as the Zuckerman report while noting that the chairman gave credit to a partly anonymous Steering Group on Scale of Enterprise for collating the information and applying their specialised knowledge to it.

There has been surprisingly scant reference to the Zuckerman report in subsequent writings on the subject of farm size and efficiency. We believe that it represents an important landmark in the development of these studies. In describing and analysing the size pattern of British agriculture, the relation of output, input and net income to farm acreage, the measurement of economic efficiency and the contribution of the farmer as a factor affecting efficiency, it paved the way not only for the subsequent series of studies which MAFF has made of the changing structure of farming but also for the important legislation foreshadowed in the White Paper on the *Development of Agriculture* which was presented to Parliament in 1965 and which, it can justly be claimed, had a powerful influence on the shaping of structural policies in other European countries.

It seemed to us that the time had come to re-examine the findings of the Zuckerman report, which related mainly to conditions in the period 1952–56, in order to see whether the situation had materially changed since its publication and at the same time to take advantage of some additional material which had become available during the intervening period.

This additional material consists of three main elements. First, the MAFF began in 1963 to classify farm size by 'standard man-days' as well as by acreage. This measurement is explained later; the point to note here is that it provided a basis for studying size and efficiency relationships which was not available to the Zuckerman Committee. For the past ten years the FMS data have been analysed in terms of standard man-days size-groups, and tables in the annual publication *Farm Incomes in England and Wales* have been in that form.

Secondly, the MAFF, as well as making its traditional annual count of the number of holdings enumerated in the June census, now divides these into some sixty size-groups in terms of standard man-days. This makes possible a very detailed analysis of the annual changes in the size-structure. Before 1962 the holdings were classified only in terms of acreage, and usually only twelve size-groups were given.

Thirdly, the use of computer tapes for both the June census and the FMS data has made it easier to obtain the various tabulations and cross-tabulations which might help to explain observed relationships and trends. By linking the standard man-days approach to the 'type-of-farming' classification system,[4] MAFF was able to proceed to a whole series of new analyses both of the census and of FMS data. These revealed hitherto unexplored features of the structure of British agriculture, and gave a new slant to the kind of questions with which the Zuckerman

3

report and other previous studies had been concerned. When we first began to make use of this facility in relation to FMS data, the latest tape available to us contained information derived from 1970–71 farm accounts. We analysed this information in considerable detail and this explains why many of the tables and graphs in this book relate to that year. Although the absolute levels of prices, value of output and expenditure were much lower in 1970–71 than they are today, it was, in retrospect, a fairly normal year. Total farm income amounted to a sum which was roughly half-way between the incomes of 1969–70 and 1971–72. It should, however, be mentioned that this was a period when agricultural production expanded fairly rapidly, and the level of productivity of labour improved substantially as the higher volume of production was achieved with a shrinking total labour force.

A word of explanation, and perhaps of apology, may be needed concerning the thick incrustation of statistical tables and graphs with which we have confronted the reader. Our defence is that we believe that all the important questions surrounding any consideration of size and efficiency are matters of degree and not of absolute and clear-cut differentiation. If anyone baldly states that 'the small farm is less efficient than the large farm' we cannot begin to attach much meaning to this unless we first have some quantitative notion of what we mean by 'small' and 'large'; of how much less efficient one is than the other; and of the proportion of instances to which the statement does or does not apply – that is, its generality in relation to all farms, to different types of farming or to different periods of time. We are dealing with indications, not with certainties, and we have tried to provide material which will enable the reader to make his own assessment of the evidence. For our part, we cannot escape from the all-pervading impression that British agriculture – and, we suspect, agriculture all over the world – is characterised by an almost imperceptible gradation from farm to farm when they are ranked in ascending or descending order in terms of size of business, productive capacity, technical performance, degree of mechanisation, managerial efficiency, profitability or almost any other feature we care to choose. This being so, we believe that the representation of approximate relationships by the use of lines and curves in diagrams is more appropriate than the construction of verbal over-simplifications which may be easily grasped but do not reflect the real situation.

The statistical approach to the study of human behaviour and social phenomena is often criticised on the grounds that it treats human beings as units, and in the process the essential individuality of each is lost.

4

Although this cannot be denied, it can be counter-argued that if we are to try to understand events which are beyond the scope of our own personal observation (which is not only limited but also highly selective), we have to make use of observations made by others. Statistics are the result of systematic generalised observation made over a wide field but focusing on certain features. Without them, the individual would be constantly open to the temptation of assuming that his own personal horizon coincided with the circumference of all human experience. It is precisely because we recognise that every individual farm is in some way a special case that we have tried in this book to emphasise that we are looking at tendencies and at the degrees of likelihood that farms of certain sizes will have certain characteristics; we have no desire to suppose a uniform pattern where none exists, to ignore the exceptional occurrence which is liable to refute any bold generalisation or to dismiss the eccentric who does not fit into our convenient categories.

Paradoxically, there may be some readers who will say that our approach has, in a sense, not been statistical enough − that we have been content to *observe* tendencies when we might have gone further to try to *explain* them by the use of multiple regression or other analytical techniques. We acknowledge that we have chosen the more limited objectives of assembling evidence about size and efficiency, suggesting some possible explanations for the apparent relationships which exist and commenting upon some of their implications for the individual farmer as well as for national agricultural policy. We hope that others will be moved to penetrate further into the causes of these relationships.

Notes

1 Levy, H. *Large and Small Holdings.* First published by Springer in Berlin, 1904. First English edition 1911. New impression 1966 published by Frank Cass.
2 Beresford has underlined the dangers of putting too much trust in figures of quantities of output.

> We are far too prone to measure productivity in quantitative terms. We should also count the cost in loss of quality. The scrupulous accountancy of nature insists on balancing the books and if we enter a credit on one side, there is usually a debit on the other. Productivity, then, on the best farms, will not be reckoned in ciphers, but by the complex and exacting scale of *progress in husbandry.*

Beresford, J. Tristram, 'The Farm as a Management Model', Special University of London Lecture, College of Estate Management, February 1970. (Reprinted in *The Estates Gazette*, 14 March 1970.)

[3] Although we make some reference to other countries, particularly in Europe, we are mainly concerned with British agriculture, and more specifically with England and Wales. This last circumscription is not made out of any disregard for the other parts of the United Kingdom (namely Scotland and Northern Ireland) but simply because the data to which we have given most consideration, conveniently available in the form we needed, are statistical data collected by the Ministry of Agriculture, Fisheries and Food (MAFF) in its Farm Management Survey (FMS) and in its agricultural censuses, both of which relate to England and Wales. We would have been happy to extend the analysis to the whole of United Kingdom had the comparable information been to hand.

[4] See Napolitan, L., and Brown, C.J. 'A type of farming classification of agricultural holdings in England and Wales according to enterprise patterns'. *Journal of Agricultural Economics,* 15(4), 1963.

2 Are Economies of Size Important in Agriculture?

The idea of 'economies of size', the meaning of which we shall examine more closely in Chapter 6, is already sufficiently well established in the vocabulary of economic discussion for us to suppose that it describes something which really exists. Experience in agriculture as well as in manufacturing industry and retail distribution has frequently confirmed that average costs per unit produced (or sold) decline as fixed costs are spread over a greater output, so that the small farm or firm with limited output but with certain unavoidable costs finds itself at a disadvantage.

Almost as much general acceptance has been given to the idea of 'diseconomies of size', which are supposed to occur once a certain size is reached and new difficulties concerning co-ordination, ease of manoeuvre, transmission of information and efficient decision-making are encountered. 'These organisational diseconomies tend increasingly to offset the force of technical economies as the scale of operation is increased.'[1]

Putting these two ideas together, there are theoretical reasons, often supported by practical experience, to suppose that below a certain (but undetermined) size, farms or firms are 'too small' to give the lowest possible cost per product unit, while above another (equally undetermined) point on the size scale, farms or firms are 'too large' and use resources less economically than they would if they were smaller.

If these simple propositions are true of British agriculture, it would seem worth trying to identify the critical points in question and to ask how many farms are of an 'uneconomic' size; what proportion of total production they embrace; whether the numbers of farms operating below the 'economic' range is increasing or diminishing; and what might be the effects on the economic efficiency of agriculture as a whole if the size-structure were to change, with or without the stimulus of government action.

If it can indeed be established beyond reasonable doubt that small farms generally use resources less efficiently than larger farms, this is likely to have important implications both for the individual farm and for the national economy, to which the agricultural sector makes a significant contribution. If the occupiers of small farms can attain a better understanding of the reasons for the relatively low return they receive from their resources — and particularly of the ways in which some small farmers have been able to surmount these difficulties — this in itself might enable them to improve their situation and to reduce the income gap which separates them from their larger neighbours. At the same time, if wider recognition of the economic handicaps of small farms leads to a more rapid reduction in their numbers and their absorption into larger units, this might bring about appreciable savings of resources which are at present deployed relatively wastefully. Thus a greater awareness of the relationship between size and efficiency might, through more efficient use of resources, benefit both the individual small farmer (or his successor) and the community as a whole. This could result either from better management of existing farms or from the better allocation of resources between farms that a different size-structure of farms would permit.

This line of argument, however, is built on certain concealed assumptions which need to be brought out into the open. In the first place, even if it can be demonstrated that small farms are generally less efficient than larger farms, in terms of the output obtained from a given amount of resources, this alone does not prove that the difference in size is the root cause of the difference in efficiency. For instance, it could well be that the managerial ability of the present occupiers of small farms is significantly lower than that of the present occupiers of larger farms — so much so that, if they were to change places, the relative efficiency of small and large farms might be reversed! Or again, it could be argued that the ascertained difference in efficiency exaggerates the apparent case for farm enlargement, because should some small farmers acquire more land and join the ranks of the larger farmers, it may not follow that they would then manage their new businesses at the higher level of efficiency currently observed among existing occupiers of the larger holdings. Some of them might find that the challenge of the new managerial tasks was beyond their capacity.

In general, differences in efficiency might well be attributable not simply to differences in size but to a whole range of other factors which happen to be associated in different degrees with small and large farms respectively.[2] Small farmers may be older; they may be less well-educated; they may attach less importance to efficiency and more to other achievements such as job satisfaction, continuity of the family tradition; they may feel that the best way of improving their prospects is to devote all their energies and waking hours to the farm without thought — or even recognition — of the cost to themselves, rather than making the most efficient use of their physical and human resources.

8

These suppositions are not fanciful; they correspond to circumstances or attitudes which have often been observed among small farmers in many countries. It follows that it may not be the shape of our agricultural structure which is to blame for differences in efficiency, but that the human factor in its present distribution tends to have different attributes in different parts of the structure. If we want to see a more efficient agricultural system and if, at the same time, many members of the farming community give, and will continue to give, higher priority to other objectives of the kinds which have been mentioned, we shall not *necessarily* improve the situation most effectively by moving as rapidly as possible towards larger farming units. It might be better, for instance, to pay more attention to improving the educational status of the occupiers of the small farms, or to providing them with better opportunities for part-time employment off the farm, than to concentrate exclusively on amalgamating small farms, even if this might assist them to achieve more fully their chosen objectives.

Efficiency and profitability

The suggestion that many farmers may not be particularly interested in efficiency as we shall be using the term is neither unrealistic nor derogatory to them. As we shall see later, a commonly accepted definition of efficiency is 'the ratio of the results achieved to the means used'.[3] If we equate 'results' with output and 'means' with input, then to be efficient is to maximise $\frac{output}{input}$. However, the great majority of farmers are not consciously aiming at a target of that kind. Their concern, so far as it can be reduced to economic terms, is much more likely to be to maximise the difference (not the ratio) between their receipts and their expenses. They want the greatest possible profit on each year's trading. The picture may be somewhat complicated by the fact that some receipts and expenses are not cash transactions (for example, the depreciation allowance is a proper item of 'expense' even though there is no annual equivalent cash payment), and receipts and expenses may not correspond exactly to 'output' and 'input' as used above. But, broadly speaking, farmers are far more interested in output minus input (i.e. profit in terms of pounds sterling) than they are in the efficiency ratio $\frac{output}{input}$, which is only a number and has no substance that can be measured in cash.[4]

A simple arithmetical example will show that the two objectives of efficiency and profitability are not identical. In terms of efficiency, it is better to achieve an output of £12,000 from an input of £10,000 than it is to achieve an output of £23,000 from an input of £20,000, because the efficiency ratio (output per unit of input) is 1·2 in the first case and 1·15 in the second; but most farmers would certainly prefer the second situation, since it leaves them with a balance of £3,000 which is a 50 per cent improvement on the balance of £2,000 which results from the first situation.

More generally, reduced profit margins per product unit are often acceptable to firms or farms which have the opportunity to enlarge the scale of their activities. A supermarket with a very large and rapid turnover may be earning high profits at a much lower efficiency ratio (output per unit of input) than is achieved by a small shop which charges higher prices on a small volume of trade.

Opportunities for greatly expanding output do not often present themselves to farmers, although there have been some spectacular instances in the poultry industry. Even so, it is reasonable for farmers to increase their input beyond the point of highest efficiency so long as the additional input costs them less (in their own estimation) than the additional output. This goes far to explain why many small farmers make such heavy demands on their own labour, a feature which will emerge prominently in the subsequent analysis.

Having indicated both the potential significance of size-and-efficiency relationships and the likelihood that the limitations of size are not the only reason for the smaller farm's lower efficiency, we may now make a brief review of the reasons which prompt us to start with the assumption that important differences in efficiency do exist between farms of different sizes, before going on to a closer examination of (i) the meaning of 'size' (Chapter 3) and 'efficiency' (Chapter 4) and (ii) the statistical evidence that a pattern of relationships can be discerned (Chapter 5).

First, there is an impressive array of statements made by authoritative writers in the field of agricultural economics. The following is a selection of these statements.

> Large farms on the average are currently more efficient than small farms. Put in another way, the good big farmer can outcompete the good little farmer. The difference between the efficiency of large farms and small farms is widening. The opportunity cost or economic penalty for operating a small farm with technology of an earlier decade is rising. The magnitude of adjustments in scale of operations necessary to produce efficiently is accelerating. Past government commodity programs appear to have abetted these conditions. (L. Quance and L.G. Tweeten in A.G. Ball and E.O. Heady (eds), *Size*,

Structure, and Future of Farms, Iowa State University Press, 1972, p. 36.)

A study of 133 farms in various parts of Britain showed that:

> productivity increased with size of farms. Although there is likely to be a limit to economies of scale, the average farm is a long way from reaching this limit ... Large size allows greater flexibility in the combination of resources and hence greater efficiency in their use. In other words larger farms suffer less from excess labour (employees and family) and under-utilisation of machinery and equipment and this tends to give them higher output per unit of input. (Economic Development Committee for Agriculture: *Farm Productivity* 1973. HMSO [for National Economic Development Office, London].)

> The only sensible measure of efficiency upon which policy conclusions can be based is a measure which takes into account *all* the resources used in relation to output ... The figures (p. 182) clearly indicate that in each of the major types of farming, the larger the size of farm the more efficiently are farming resources used ... Therefore, any move towards the amalgamation of farms and an increase in the size of the operating unit should apparently increase the efficiency of the industry as a whole. (H.T. Williams, *Principles for British Agricultural Policy,* OUP, 1960.)

> The existing structure [of Swedish agriculture], with its small acreages (mean acreage 19hs.) and small herds (average 8 cows and 30 pigs) does not admit of anything like the optimum factor proportions in agriculture. (O. Gulbrandsen and A. Lindbeck, *The Economics of the Agricultural Sector,* The Industrial Institute for Economic and Social Research, Stockholm, 1973.)

Secondly, we may quote the evidence produced by the above-mentioned Zuckerman Committee, which was summarised in the following statement reproduced from the report:

> When the value of the farmer's own labour is taken into account small farms are on the average less economic in their production than large farms: their total costs are greater per £100 of output produced.

This statement is supported by Figure 5.2 which is also taken from the Zuckerman report.

Opinion on this matter, however, is far from being unanimous. Many statements could be quoted which cast doubt on the validity or generality

11

of the principle of economies of size when applied to agriculture. Maunder[3] remarked that while 'it is generally agreed that the efficiency of industrial undertakings increases with size, at least up to a point . . . so far as agriculture is concerned there is a good deal of difference of opinion.' Here are some statements which tend to strengthen the doubts:

For Irish farms in general, at the factor prices applied in this study, larger farms tend to be more efficient than smaller ones but the results are not fully conclusive. (B.C. Hickey, 'Economies of Size in Irish Farming', *Irish J. Agric. Econ. Rur. Sociol.* vol. 3, no. 1, 1970.)

The family farm structure would be threatened if scale or cost economies extended over large acreages. We believe, and have supporting empirical evidence that this is not the case . . . Substantial cost economies can result from some further expansion of small or modal sized farms. However, because variable costs of the agricultural firm eventually dominate total costs, cost reductions per acre eventually become minute as acreage continues to expand with a given power and machinery unit. When this point has been reached, no great cost advantage is realised by a larger unit. (E.O. Heady, *Agricultural Policy under Economic Development,* Iowa State Univ. Press, 1962.)

The fully mechanised one-man farm captures most of the economies associated with size – from the standpoint of costs per unit. (W.R. Bailey, *The One-Man Farm,* US Dept of Agriculture, Econ. Research Service 519, August 1973.)

If cost economies of size do exist, how large does a farm have to become before the cost economies are exhausted? Madden has summarized past research in this area. The results of this study indicate that when a crop farm attains a one-man to two-man operation, it has realized all the cost economies of size. (D.O. Anderson 'Economic Means of Farm Groups', (Chapter 19 in A.G. Ball and E.O. Heady (eds), *Size, Structure and Future of Farms,* Iowa State University Press, 1972.)

Most machine processes in agriculture require only one or two persons to operate them efficiently . . . farm operations are as widely separated by time intervals after mechanisation as before . . . The advantages of large-scale production, consequently, are much less important in agriculture than in industry. On the other hand the greater difficulty of management in agriculture than in industry as the size of business is increased becomes much more important at a smaller size. This is due to the much greater time and space dimensions of the production process in agriculture and to the much greater variation in practices required to fit the production process to variations in soils, weather and the characteristics of plants and animals . . .

The small farm supported by a network of government and other institutions performing the relatively few functions that require large-scale organisations has proved to be efficient. (K.L. Bachman and R.P. Christensen.)[2]

A general overview of evidence from a number of rural industries [i.e. types of farming] in Australia has been provided by Mackay. His scatter diagrams . . . led him to conclude that 'These observations strongly suggest that long-run average cost curves for rural industries commonly are strongly downward sloping over the lower ranges of farm size and that thereafter unit costs remain more or less constant'. However, some of the evidence . . . is unconvincing . . . Research should endeavour to establish whether small farms are high cost because of the nature of economies of size (doubtful, because of the simultaneous existence of low-cost small farms), the use of inferior technologies (a possible explanation), type of cost accounting procedures employed (a possible explanation) or some combination of all these factors (the most likely explanation). (J.R. Anderson and R.A. Powell, 'Economies of Size in Australian Farming', *Austral. Jour. of Ag. Econs.*, vol. 17, no. 1, April 1973.)

These differing points of view make it clear that there are unresolved questions and some apparently contradictory or inconsistent evidence which indicates a need for further analysis. Underlying them all is the feeling that the issue has profound implications for agricultural policy and for the incomes of farm people.

Notes

[1] Moore, J.B. *An Introduction to Modern Economic Theory*, The Free Press (New York, 1973).

[2] It has been remarked, in relation to developing countries, that:

... the apparent differences in resource productivity associated with size turn out upon further analysis to be correlated with land use, type of farming, capital availability, land tenure and other factors that may or may not be associated with size in specific situations.

Barraclough, S.L. commenting on Bachman, K.L. and Christensen, R.P., 'The Economics of Farm Size', Chapter 7 in *Agricultural Development and Economic Growth,* ed. Southworth, H.F., and Johnston, B.F. Cornell Univ. Press (1967).

[3] Maunder, A.H. *Size and Efficiency in Farming,* Institute for Research in Agricultural Economics, Oxford 1952, p. 9.

[4] 'The chief incentive for farm enlargement ... is not to reduce unit costs of production, but to achieve a larger business, more output and more total income.' Bailey, W.R., *The One-Man Farm,* US Dept of Ag. (1973).

3 The Measurement of Size and Size Distributions

Alternative measures of size

In the past, farm size has commonly been taken to be synonymous with farm acreage. However, when it becomes necessary to specify the criterion of size, in making a judgement between farm businesses, acreage is soon shown to be a rather unsatisfactory indicator of business size. This is because the proportions in which land and the other factors (labour, capital and so forth) combine together in production vary, principally between types of farming, but also between farms of the same type.

The 'best' unit of measurement of farm size, and also of the size of enterprises within farms, will depend very much on the purpose for which the measurement is to be used. To a geographer or planner concerned with the use of the countryside and its allocation between farming, forestry and recreation for townsfolk, the most appropriate measure might be acreage. If he considers land only in terms of the space it provides, a large farm to him will imply one which covers a lot of land in the same way as large forests or parks will be those which extend over many acres.

When farms are considered as businesses, however, acreage no longer remains the most appropriate measure. Farm businesses collectively form one of the sectors of the economy which together generate the national income. This national income is usually taken as the money value of all the goods and services produced and consumed by society's economic activity during a year. The contribution which each firm makes to the national income can be measured by its 'value added'; this is the value of each firm's output *less* the value of goods which the firm buys from other firms. For example, a farm might calculate its 'value added' by subtracting from the total value of its sales the cost of the other goods and services it buys from other firms — its expenditure on fertilizers, fuel, veterinary bills and so forth. Machinery and other capital equipment does not all wear out in a single year, so its value is spread out, or depreciated, over a number of years and an estimate for one year's share deducted in the process of calculating what is known as 'net value added'.

'Value added', then, is a measure of the farm's contribution to national income, generated by the land, labour, capital and management on the farm. Furthermore, wages, rent, interest and profit have to come out of the reward earned by these factors. From the national point of view, 'value added' is probably the best way of measuring the size of any business, but it is not yet widely used in relation to the agricultural industry because survey data showing 'values added' for individual farms are not readily available.

Available measures of size

The most commonly used measures of business size can be divided into those which are calculated on input and those calculated on output. Among the measurements of *input* are farm acreage (the input of land), standard man-days (the theoretically required input of labour), the value of capital tied up in the business, and the value of all the inputs used in a year. Among the measurements of *output* are physical data, such as the number of eggs or broilers produced per year on a poultry holding, or value data, such as the total value of milk sold from a dairy farm. 'Gross output' and 'net output', as used by the Ministry of Agriculture in its series of reports on farm incomes in England and Wales, have special meanings and are part way between the value of the farm's total output and 'value added' — 'gross output' being the value of total output less livestock and livestock products bought from other farms, and 'net output' being 'gross output' less the cost of purchased seeds and feedstuffs.

Official statistics concentrate at present on acreage and standard labour requirements — that is, land and labour inputs — as the principal measures of farm size. Farm acreage could be taken as an acceptable indicator of business size if one could be sure that all the other factors of production were linked in an unvarying way with acreage. Perhaps this occurs within certain farming types; for example, it might be reasonable to state that a 500-acre cereal farm was twice the size of a 250-acre cereal farm if the larger one also used twice the number of tractors and labour units, twice the quantity of fertilizer and so on. However, we may well find that *output* and acreage do not increase proportionally, so that a farm which is double the size in terms of acreage and all other inputs is often *less* than double the size in terms of output. One of our main purposes is to examine how the efficiency of factor use varies with size of business — however the latter is defined.

Acreage is particularly misleading when used as basis for comparing farms of different types. When measured in any way other than by acreage, a lowland dairy farm of 100 acres may be a much larger business than a hill-land sheep farm consisting of 300 acres of rough grazing — it may have a higher value of output or input, employ more labour and so on. Soil quality and location obviously affect the quantity of other factors used with land and also the output achieved from them. Variations in soil quality, however, can be partly counteracted by expressing acreages of rough grazing in terms of the number of lowland pasture acres of equivalent productive capacity to give an 'adjusted' acreage for the farm. In some studies, the variation in soil quality has been allowed for by measuring the farm's total land value or rental value in substitution for acreage, although this too is imperfect in that such values are influenced by other factors besides soil quality.

Standard man-days

The standard labour requirement of a farm (in standard man-days or smd's) is an alternative measure of size which has the advantage of taking into account the intensity of land use. It is based on estimates of the annual requirements of manual labour 'needed *on average* for the production of crops and livestock with an addition for essential maintenance and other necessary tasks'.[1] A single smd represents 8 hours manual work for an adult male worker under average conditions.

No one would claim that smd's are the perfect or the sole valid measurement of business size; the main reason for their use is simply that, for most purposes, they are less distorting than a measure based on acreage. Smd's reflect the intensity with which land is farmed and hence, indirectly, its quality — a small acreage intensive dairy farm may well be ranked higher than an extensive ranch-type beef holding. As this example also illustrates, they permit comparisons between farms of different types; a comparison between a cereal farm and a horticultural holding would be meaningless in terms of business size if it were made solely in terms of acreage.

Smd's are also more closely linked to most other measures of business size, such as the annual value of output or the cost of inputs, than is acreage.[2] While these other measures are preferable, they are not widely available; smd's form a valuable proxy.

The smd requirements estimated for individual farms will not necessarily correspond to the actual labour available on those farms. Smd's are based on average requirements, around which individual farms will range.

17

Because labour often comes in 'blocks' of one man, a particular farm may find that, although it is overmanned, cutting the labour force would make the concern non-viable. This happens in particular on small family farms where perhaps the entire labour force consists of a farmer and his son — both may be under-employed but the departure of either would make operations requiring two people impossible. On the other hand smd's will sometimes overestimate the quantity actually used, particularly where an above-average quantity of machinery is employed. By taking account of the differing quantities of capital between farms, discrepancies between the actual amount of labour employed and the estimated 'standard' requirements might be greatly reduced. A correction of this kind is seldom feasible, however, and a comparison of smd estimates and actual labour employed, while giving an indication of the divergence of the labour productivity on a particular farm from the norm, is no guide to the overall efficiency of that farm.

Techniques of production change with time, generally requiring a smaller labour force, so it is to be expected that the periodic revisions of national smd's, which are undertaken to keep them in line with actual average labour requirements, should normally be downwards. Such revisions would progressively reduce a farm's total smd on a given amount of cropping and stocking, but would not imply a shrinking in the size of the business in terms of value of output, combined value of inputs or in 'value added.' Smd's can only be used to make size-of-business comparisons between different time periods if standard labour requirements remain constant. While revisions to accommodate changing techniques will indicate the enterprises in which output per man is increasing most, they must not be taken as representing changes in overall business efficiency.

The expression 'standard man-days' has not yet been universally adopted into the vocabulary of the farming community. It has an air of abstraction and contrivance which is quite absent from the homely word 'acre', which has come down to us from time immemorial. Moreover, it seems unlikely that this expression has found a permanent place even in the language of agricultural statisticians and economists. One consequence of Britain's membership of the EEC has been the necessity to conform, as far as possible, to the Community's formally adopted statistical definitions. It is understood that for the purpose of classifying farms by size the Community is likely to settle for a measure related to the net value of output after the cost of certain inputs has been deducted, in which case recourse will presumably be made to 'standard net output,' 'standard gross margin' or some such term. If the annual census of British agriculture had included questions about receipts and expenses, as is the case in some countries, it is likely that standard man-days would never have been invented and we would have been spared the use of such an unfamiliar term. Whether the term will completely disappear from British agricultural statistics remains to be seen; but as it has been used without interruption (though with modification) for twelve years, no one who is interested in structural analysis and policy can ignore its existence.

Relationship between size of farm in acres and size of farm business in standard man-days

Because these two alternative measures of size are in frequent use, it is interesting to recognise the relationship between them. To what extent is a farm's acreage a reliable indicator of its size of business, and vice versa? And is the relationship constant regardless of size, or does it vary as one moves along the size scale?

Table 3.1
Acreage of crops and grass associated with different levels of size of business, England and Wales, 1972

Size of business (smd)	Acres (crops and grass)			Median $\div$ Q_1	Q_3 $\div$ Median
	First quartile	Median	Third quartile		
175–224	19	38	65	2·00	1·72
275–324	29	54	86	1·84	1·58
375–424	37	69	97	1·86	1·41
475–524	54	84	126	1·54	1·51
575–624	62	96	141	1·56	1·46
675–724	72	114	163	1·60	1·43
750–849	78	128	187	1·64	1·46
850–949	95	142	207	1·50	1·46
1,000–1,099	113	168	247	1·50	1·47
1,500–1,799	162	259	366	1·59	1·42
2,400–2,699	210	398	632	1·89	1·59
3,900–4,199	229	551	856	2·41	1·55
4,500–4,799	264	613	961	2·32	1·57
5,100–5,699	252	669	—	2·65	—
6,000–7,999	258	734	—	2·85	—

Source: Derived from MAFF Table 902, June 1972 Census.

Table 3.2
Size of business associated with different sizes of farm, England and Wales, June 1972

Size of farm (acres, crops and grass)	Standard man-days			Median $\div$ Q_1	Q_3 $\div$ Median
	First quartile	Median	Third quartile		
20—49·75	80	172	321	2·15	1·87
50—99·75	264	414	590	1·57	1·43
100—149·75	455	642	872	1·41	1·36
150—199·75	617	853	1,148	1·38	1·35
200—299·75	809	1,104	1,478	1·36	1·34
300—399·75	1,092	1,463	1,972	1·34	1·35
400—499·75	1,387	1,853	2,470	1·34	1·33
500—999·75	2,028	2,719	3,711	1·34	1·36

Source: Derived from MAFF Table 902, June 1972 Census.

The MAFF prepares an annual table from the agricultural census returns, showing the distribution over the smd size-groups of the holdings in each acreage size-group (Table 902 in the MAFF series). From the June 1972 analysis, the relationships shown in Tables 3.1 and 3.2 and Figures 3.1 and 3.2 can be derived. The value of 25 per cent of the holdings in the group in question comes below the value represented by the first quartile; 25 per cent are above the third quartile; and 50 per cent occur above and below the median value. Table 3.1 and Figure 3.1 show that the median acreage rises steadily as size of business increases, but there is considerable and regular variation around the median. For instance, at 800 smd's the median size in 1972 was 128 acres, but 50 per cent of businesses at this level were outside the range of 78—187 acres. The ratios between the median acreage and the respective quartiles were highest at the extremes of size of business, but in no group was there a ratio of less than 1·42.

Table 3.2 shows that acreage is a somewhat more reliable indicator of size of business than was given by the converse relationship analysed in Table 3.1. In the smallest size-group shown (20—49·75 acres) half the farms fell outside the range of 80—321 smd, but, after the 100 acre point is passed, the variation is reduced and the ratios between the median and the quartiles fall to about 1·35 and remain close to that value. Figure 3.2 shows what levels of size of business are to be found in association with various acreage sizes. Here again, it will be seen that the relationship and the variation around it follow a regular pattern.

These tables and graphs serve to demonstrate that these two aspects of size must not be expected to correspond at all closely on individual farms, even though *on average* there is a strikingly regular relationship.

It must also be remembered that, as successive years bring improvements in the productivity of labour, this relationship is changing — in absolute numerical terms if not in its general shape — so that given acreages of crops or numbers of livestock can be tended with fewer days of work. If the intensification of farming systems was fully compensating for this reduction in labour requirements (per unit of crops and stock),

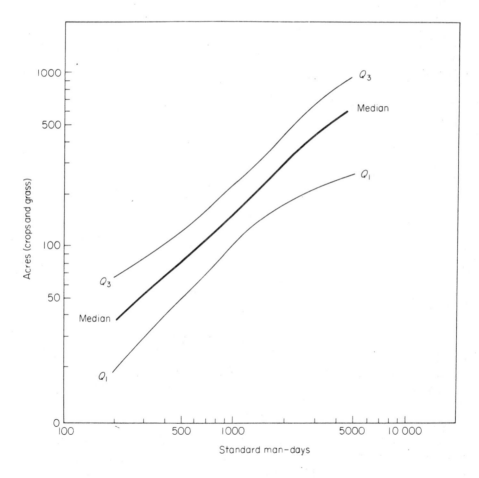

Fig. 3.1 Acres of crops and grass associated with different levels of size of business, England and Wales, 1972

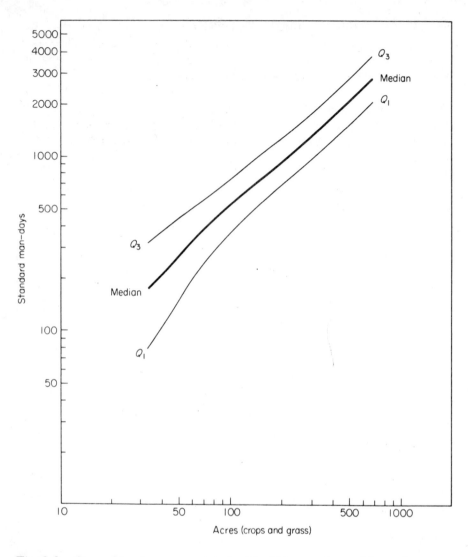

Fig. 3.2   Size of business associated with different sizes of farm, England and Wales, June 1972

farms of a given acreage would continue to require as much labour as before, but in fact this has not been the case. Table 3.3 shows that between 1967 and 1972 there was a reduction in standard labour requirements at all levels of acreage-size. Thus, a 300-acre farm, for example, required an average of 1,400 man-days of labour in 1967, but only 1,300 in 1972 — a reduction of about 7 per cent. This was the net effect of both the reduction in the smd coefficients used by MAFF, the increase in livestock numbers and (in some cases) the change in the cropping pattern towards more labour-intensive crops.

Table 3.3
Change between 1967 and 1972 in the median number of
standard man-days associated with different sizes of farm

Size of farm (acres, crops and grass)	Standard man-days		1972 as per cent of 1967
	1967	1972	
20—49·75	224	172	76·8
50—99·75	461	414	89·8
100—149·75	704	642	91·2
150—199·75	917	853	93·0
200—299·75	1,183	1,104	93·3
300—399·75	1,570	1,463	93·2
400—499·75	1,981	1,853	93·5
500—999·75	2,853	2,719	95·3

Present size-structure of agriculture in England and Wales

If there are important differences in average efficiency between farms of different sizes, the question arises: what proportion of the total agricultural resources, in terms of land, labour and capital, is absorbed by farms in the different size-groups? In particular, what proportion is taken up by the size-groups which are of lower efficiency than the rest? It may also be asked: what additional output or what saving in inputs would be achieved if the level of efficiency in the size-groups with the poorest economic performance could be raised to the average of the other groups?

Statistics derived from the annual agricultural census make it possible to study the distribution of land, livestock, labour and other agricultural items between farms of different sizes. Some of these statistics are published in MAFF's series entitled *Farm Classification in England and Wales;* others have appeared in other MAFF publications from time to time, notably in *The Changing Structure of Agriculture* (1970); and others are available in the annual *Agricultural Statistics* or from MAFF's Agricultural Censuses and Surveys Branch on request.

At this point it is necessary to refer to an awkward feature of the statistics which is liable to give rise to wrong conclusions if it is overlooked, namely that not all of the agricultural holdings enumerated in the census are separate farms. There are many instances of 'multiple holdings', where two or more holdings are under the same management but for which separate returns are rendered to the MAFF. This may be a legacy of the past, in that the *de facto* amalgamation of holdings into one unit has not been notified to the Ministry — perhaps because the holdings are physically separated, although combined for management purposes. For several years, the Ministry has been endeavouring to improve the accuracy of its statistics by requesting occupiers to return on one form figures for holdings which are farmed together. In this way, 'statistical' amalgamations are catching up with the actual changes in farm size which have already occurred. During certain years, the MAFF was particularly active in this operation; for instance, the statistics show that between 1970 and 1971 about 10,000 holdings disappeared because they were returned as part of a larger unit instead of separately as before.[3] This process of statistical amalgamation has still quite a long way to go. Harrison[4] has estimated that, in England, the number of farms over 5 acres in 1969 was only about 85 per cent of the number of holdings enumerated in the census of that year. This figure is an overstatement of the number of farms of under 100 acres and an understatement of the number of farms of over 300 acres.

This section deals with the statistics of holdings, and should be interpreted accordingly. As they are so readily accessible, the basic statistics are not reproduced here,[5] but the distribution of land and of labour requirement (smd) is shown graphically in Figures 3.3 and 3.4. These are in the form of cumulative percentage distributions, in order to answer the question: how much of the land (or the labour requirement) is to be found on holdings of below a certain size, or within a certain size range, or above a certain size?

Figure 3.3, then, shows that in England and Wales in 1973 holdings of under 100 acres accounted for 20 per cent of the total crops and grass acreage; holdings of 100 to 300 acres contained about 39 per cent (59 minus 20); and holdings of over 300 acres had 41 per cent. A logarithmic scale has been used on the horizontal axis in this and in many of the succeeding diagrams, in order to accommodate what would otherwise be a very long tail to the distribution.

The dotted line on the graph shows the distribution of standard man-days between holdings of different acreages. This can be regarded as roughly equivalent to the distribution of output of agricultural products

24

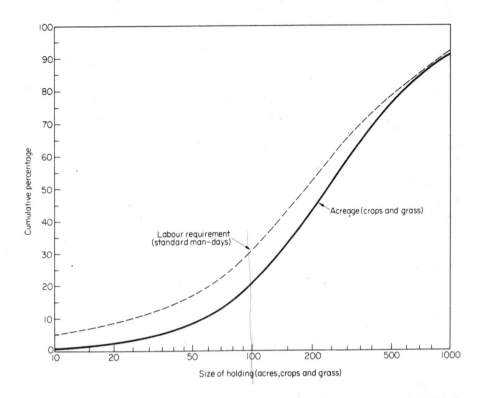

Fig. 3.3 Cumulative percentage distribution of acreage and labour requirement by size of farm, England and Wales, 1973

by size of holding, since smd's are based on the quantities of the various crops and kinds of livestock which are recorded on each holding, and the output is fairly closely related to the labour required to tend them. From this dotted line, it can be deduced that holdings of under 100 acres are responsible for about 30 per cent of the total agricultural output. This, it will be seen, is more than their proportion of the land area, because smaller holdings make more intensive use of the land. Farms of between 100 and 300 acres account for some 35 per cent of total output (65 minus 30); and those above 300 acres, 35 per cent.

If studies of size and efficiency lead to the conclusion that we have a structural problem in British agriculture, this graph may help to assess the extent of the problem if it can be identified as being mainly associated with farms within a given size range.

Figure 3.4 presents the same kind of analysis, but in this case the size of holding is measured in terms of smd (size of business). We can see that

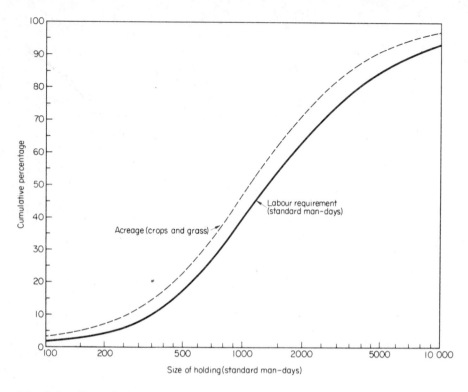

Fig. 3.4 Cumulative percentage distribution of acreage and labour requirement by size of business, England and Wales, 1971

holdings of less than 600 smd's account for about 22 per cent of the total labour requirement (which again we may regard as giving a fair indication of the proportion of total output which these holdings contribute) and about 28 per cent of the land. (Small businesses evidently use their land rather less intensively than large businesses; they include, for instance, many beef and sheep farms which have relatively small numbers of livestock on a rather extensive acreage.) At the other end of the scale, the large farms of 3,000 smd or more (that is, employing about 10 full-time workers or more, in addition to the farmer) account for 25 per cent of total output and 17 per cent of the land.

One advantage of this way of presenting the data is that the graphs are largely unaffected by the inclusion or exclusion of numbers of very small holdings. From time to time, census definitions have been altered so that thousands of holdings which had hitherto been required to make returns of their land and livestock were exempted on the grounds that their holdings were 'statistically insignificant' and not worth the considerable trouble (to both the Ministry and the occupier) of enumeration. If figures of 'average size' of holding are being calculated, the inclusion or omission of these thousands of small holdings will materially affect the results, but, in the circumstances described, Figures 3.3 and 3.4 would register only minor adjustments at the bottom left-hand corner of each diagram.

These distributions change from year to year, but not very dramatically. In Figure 3.3, the lines should be imagined as moving gradually downwards towards the horizontal axis. In other words, a diminishing proportion of land and labour requirement is to be found on the smaller holdings year by year. To a lesser extent, this is also true of Figure 3.4 as farm businesses tend to increase in size.

The fact that relatively small farms still very much predominate in numbers, if not in total land area, is depicted in Figure 3.5. This represents an adaptation of the traditional size-group table which shows the number of holdings in each of a limited number of groups of varying size-ranges. It converts the same basic data into the number of holdings which are estimated to fall within each 50-acre size interval, and the total number of acres which those successive numbers of holdings contain. It illustrates the following features of British agriculture.

1   The larger the size of holding, the fewer are the holdings to be found of that size. This is evidently a regular and systematic relationship; there is no 'bunching' at certain levels of size such as might have been expected if, at some point in history (as occurred over larger areas of the United States), land had been parcelled out in standard-sized units.
2   The amount of land to be found in successive 50-acre size intervals increases steadily up to a maximum of about 3 million acres which is recorded on holdings of 50 to 100 acres. Although there are more holdings of under 50 acres, they account for a smaller total land area than holdings of 50 to 100 acres. (In statistical terms, although the mode of the holdings distribution is very small and certainly below 20 acres – its precise location depending on the definition of 'holding' for census purposes – the mode of the acreage distribution lies at about 90 acres. In other words, an acre of farm land chosen at random is more likely to be on a holding of 90 acres than on a holding of any other size, the probabilities varying according to the shape of the lower line in Figure 3.5.)

Any structural change towards the enlargement of farms and the reduction in their total number lowers the 'number of holdings' line in Figure 3.5 at its left-hand end and raises it at its right-hand end. In other

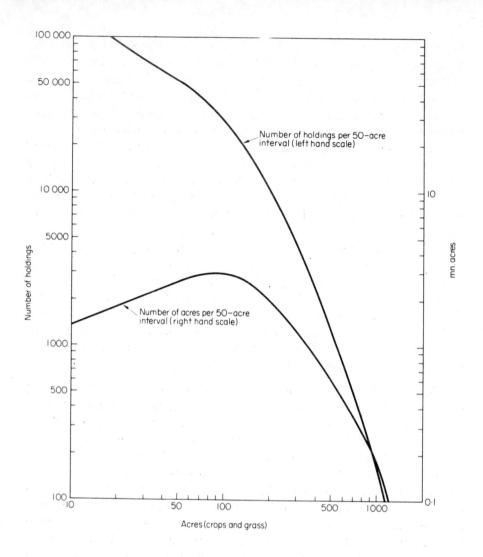

Fig. 3.5 Distribution of holdings and acres by 50-acre intervals centred at different acreage sizes, England and Wales, 1973

The relationship between the two lines on the graph is that for any given acreage on the horizontal scale, the number of acres (read from the right-hand scale) divided by the number of holdings (read from the left-hand scale) equals the acreage in question.

words, the 'pyramid' structure of agriculture, with its great number of small farms and its very few large farms, is gradually becoming less broadly based. The peak of the 'number of acres' curve in the same diagram is slowly shifting to the right.

Figure 3.6 treats the distribution of holdings by standard man-day (size of business) groups in the same way as Figure 3.5 deals with holdings in acreage intervals. It shows once again that the smaller the farm business, the more numerous the businesses are, but the shape of the distribution is noticeably different. For instance, there are nearly as many holdings of 350–400 smd's as there are holdings of 250–300 smd's. However, above the size of about 550 smd's (the '2-man' farm) the successive numbers in size groups of equal interval fall off quite rapidly.

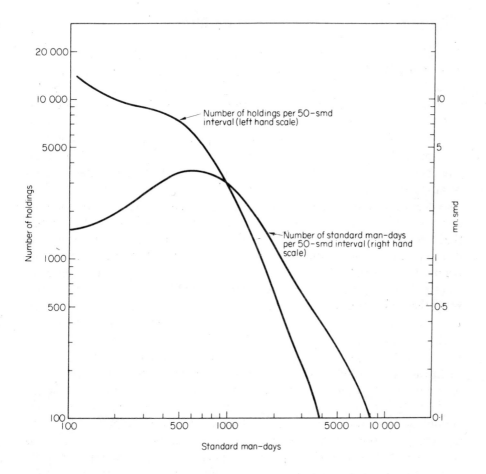

Fig. 3.6   Distribution of holdings and standard man-days by 50-smd intervals centred at different smd sizes, England and Wales, 1973

The peak of the 'number of smd' curve appears to come at a business size of about 550 smd. In other words, there is more total agricultural productive activity taking place on 2-man holdings (say 525–575 smd) than at any other size-interval of equal range. This gives substance to the picture of British agriculture as an industry still dominated by family-sized businesses, both in numbers and in the sense that if a measured unit of agricultural activity (producing crops and/or livestock) is pinpointed at random, it is more likely to be found on the 2-man farm than at any other single size-level.

Differential rates of change in the size-structure

Recognising that farm incomes generally increase with the size of farm (see Figure 5.9), it is only to be expected that many farmers will have been looking for opportunities to enlarge the scope of their activities, by acquiring more land, intensifying production on their existing area, or both. Some correspondence should therefore be found between differences in profitability between size-groups and changes in the numbers of farms in the respective groups. If small businesses have to struggle to keep going, one would expect their number to gradually decline and the numbers of farms at or above the economically viable size to increase.

Indeed, this line of approach could be followed further. If economies of size are very much in evidence up to a certain level of size, but beyond that point they diminish, eventually ceasing or even becoming diseconomies of size, then it might be expected that the pressure of competition for land and for agricultural resources would generally squeeze out the smallest businesses most rapidly, the somewhat larger businesses less rapidly and so on, until a size could be identified at which the numbers of businesses being absorbed into larger, more economic units were just about balanced by the numbers which were attaining that size by the process of absorption of smaller units. There would be a kind of 'break-even' or 'dead centre' point indicating a general ability to survive at that size. If there is, even in a very general and qualified way, a recognisable optimum size of farm, trends in the size distribution of farms should show an increase in the number of farms of this optimum size and a decrease in the numbers of farms not conforming with that size. If, as we believe, the notion of an optimum size is dubious in agriculture but the notion of a minimum size for economic viability is more acceptable, then trends should show a decrease in the number of farms below that size and an increase in the numbers above it.

This approach has been termed the 'survivorship technique', and has been pursued in some American studies.[5] It has been pointed out, however, that the profit-maximising size is greater than the highest efficiency (lowest-average-cost-of-production) size because profits continue to accrue even with rising average cost, so long as the price of the product is still higher than marginal cost. For this reason 'we should expect farm operations to gravitate towards sizes well beyond the most efficient size'.[6]

It must also be remembered that there is an inevitable time-lag, which may cover many years and even a whole generation, between a farm family's recognition of the need to enlarge their business and the realisation of that objective. The land market is such that it may be a long time before adjacent land becomes available for purchase or rent. The alternative of moving to a larger farm may present formidable problems. This chronic immobility of farm resources may be reinforced by economic uncertainties or social maladjustments, so that the adjustment of the actual farm structure to the ideal pattern, which could be postulated on the basis of the available technology and managerial ability, is likely to be a hesitant and fitful process, only very partially and imperfectly achieved.

Superimposed on all this is the fact that the optimum size of the minimum size for viability will itself be changing as new techniques are adopted, new forms of integration (horizontal and vertical) are taken up and higher levels of managerial ability are attained. To quote only one example, Shepherd[7] has pointed out that, in 1950, the most efficient size of farm under typical conditions in Iowa was about 240 acres. By 1960, with new machinery available, the most efficient size was 360 acres. Yet, in 1960, most Iowa farms constituted much less, the average for that year being about 192 acres (including pasture land). They could have operated at the most efficient size without necessarily ceasing to be family farms, but the process of structural adjustment, though seemingly inexorable, was slow.

British data are available which lend themselves to this 'differential rate of survival' approach, and Figures 3.7 and 3.8 summarise the situation as it has appeared in recent years. The system of presentation is to show, for successive size-groups, the number of holdings enumerated in a given year expressed as a percentage of the number enumerated in the same size-group in an earlier year.[8] Thus the percentage will indicate a rate of disappearance or (if it is over 100) a rate of increase.

Figure 3.7 shows that the number of holdings of about 30 acres declined by about 30 per cent between 1963 and 1973. Moving up the scale to holdings of about 100 acres, the rate of decline was about 20 per

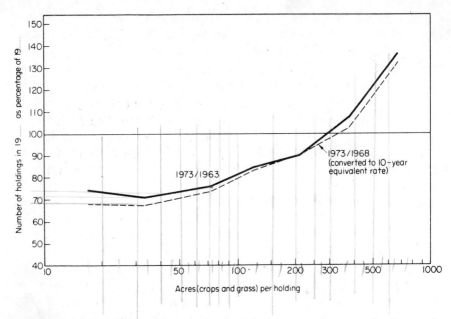

Fig. 3.7 Relationship between size of holding and rate of change in number of holdings of that size, England and Wales, 1963, 1968 and 1973

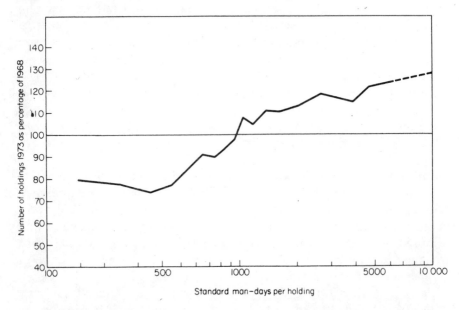

Fig. 3.8 Relationship between size of farm business and rate of change in number of holdings of that size, England and Wales, 1968 and 1973

cent; at 200 acres, it was about 10 per cent; and at 300 acres, there was no decline at all, the numbers remaining constant. In the same period, however, farms of 500 acres increased in number by 21 per cent and farms of 600 acres by 30 per cent. The regularity with which the rates of change vary according to size is striking.

The dotted line in Figure 3.7 presents the same kind of analysis but for the more recent five-year period, 1968–73. The interesting features are that (1) the disappearance of small holdings has tended to accelerate, being more rapid in the last five years than in the ten-year period of which they are part; and (2) that the 'watershed' size of farm – corresponding to the point below which numbers of holdings tend to decline and above which they tend to increase – has moved up, from 300 acres in the ten-year period to about 350 acres in the more recent five years. This conforms fully to theoretical expectations.

Figure 3.8 shows the results of a similar analysis, but using smd as the measure of size instead of acreage. During the period covered (1968–73) MAFF did not revise its labour requirement standards, so the yardstick of farm business size remains unchanged. The picture closely resembles that of Figure 3.7. Small farm businesses of less than 500 smd's (that is, farms requiring less than two full-time people to operate them) declined in number over the five years by more than 20 per cent. Farms of over 1,000 smd's increased in number, and, generally speaking, the larger the size the more rapid the increase in numbers. It appears that the balancing point, at which numbers neither declined nor increased, occurred at just under 1,000 smd during this period – that is, at somewhere between the 3-man and the 4-man farm.

It is interesting to find that the same pattern of structural change is occurring in other countries. Figures 3.9 and 3.10 relate to the Netherlands and Figure 3.11 to Germany (Federal Republic). Figure 3.9 shows that, in the Netherlands, in the period 1959 to 1965, farms of less than 13 ha. were declining in number while larger farms were tending to increase. Both these tendencies became much more marked in the subsequent five years from 1965 to 1970, when the number of holdings of less than 4 ha. declined sharply. As in England and Wales, it is evident that the 'break-even' point moved upwards, from 13 ha. to 17 ha., confirming the impression that the economically viable size is a dynamic rather than a static concept.

Figure 3.10 for the Netherlands corresponds to Figure 3.8 for England and Wales in that it is concerned with size of business as measured in standard labour requirements. In the relatively short space of three years, the numbers of holdings requiring less than 1½ man-years of labour fell by

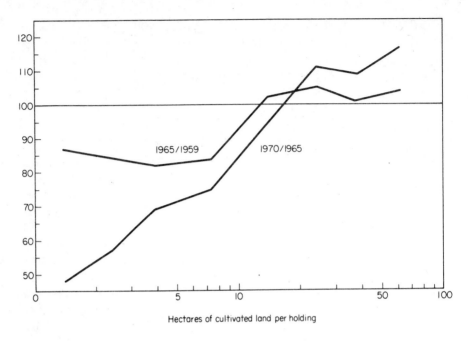

Fig. 3.9 Relationship between size of holding and rate of change in number of holdings of that size, Netherlands, 1959, 1965 and 1970

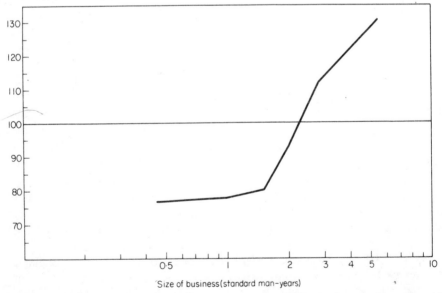

Fig. 3.10 Relationship between size of farm business and rate of change in number of holdings of that size, Netherlands, 1965 and 1968

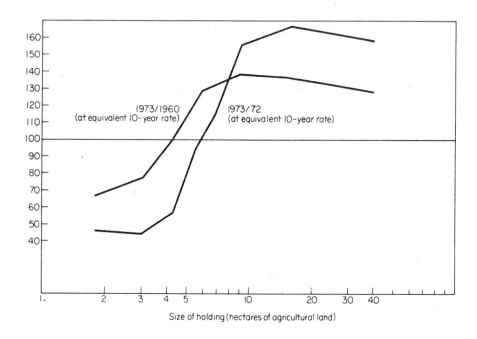

Fig. 3.11 Relationship between size of holding and rate of change in number of holdings of that size, Federal Republic of Germany, 1960, 1972 and 1973

over 20 per cent, while there was a rapid increase in holdings requiring 4 man-years or more. The balancing point came at about 2¼ man-years, which is lower than in England and Wales. However, this is not surprising when we realise that the present structure of Dutch agriculture is dominated by much smaller holdings.

Figure 3.11 tells much the same story for agriculture in the Federal Republic of Germany. Comparison of the two lines in the diagram shows that small holdings have been disappearing at an accelerating rate and the rate of amalgamation into holdings of 10 ha. or more (which is relatively large by German standards) has also been increasing. The 'break-even' point in 1972–73 appears to have been at about 6 ha., compared with just over 4 ha. in the period 1960–73. One difference, however, to be noted between the German situation and that of the Netherlands and of England and Wales is that, in the case of Germany, it does not appear to follow that the larger the size, the more rapid the increase in numbers. The number of farms over 10 ha. shows no general tendency to increase and may even seem to decline, even though these holdings are certainly increasing in absolute numbers.

Use of Farm Management Survey data to estimate the size-distribution of output, input, net income and tenant's capital in England and Wales

Having looked at the distribution of land and of total labour requirements between farms of different sizes, and having analysed trends in the size-distribution itself, we now turn from census data to economic data as collected annually in the Farm Management Survey from a sample of about 2,500 farms and attempt to find out what proportion of the national agricultural output, input, net income and tenant's capital is to be found in the different size-groups — *a question which is of special interest if some of these groups generally operate at lower levels of efficiency than others.* By making use of the FMS sample data on output and inputs within the respective size-groups and combining this with census data indicating the relative importance of the different size-groups (in smd or acreage terms), it is possible to build up estimates of the distribution of output and inputs between farms of different sizes in agriculture as a whole.

This process of estimating the total picture from the evidence of the sample presupposes that the sample is sufficiently representative for this purpose. This may not be so. In *Farm Incomes in England and Wales 1970—71* (p. 8) it is stated that 'the sample contains proportionately more of the larger businesses of 1,200 to 4,199 smd and fewer in the 275—299 smd group compared with the distribution of the total population of farms in the Census'. The same statement has been repeated in subsequent issues of the series. However, reference to the census figures giving the size distribution of the whole 'population' of holdings makes it possible, by appropriate weighting, to overcome satisfactorily this known bias in the FMS towards larger farms. No such control is possible on the sample measurements of output or input in value terms, as these items are not collected in the census.

However, one further check is possible, revealing another degree of correspondence between the sample and the population, namely the intensity of farming within each size-group. The census tables can be used to derive information on the number of smd per acre, (in each size-of-business group, type-of-farming group and region if required) and, by comparing this with the figures from the FMS for any specified size-group, it is possible to see whether the FMS sample is composed of farms which, on average, have about the same intensity of cropping and stocking as is to be found among all farms of that group. In this way, any suggestion that the FMS farms are consistently chosen from among the more 'productive' farms (in the sense of having more livestock per acre and more labour-intensive cropping per acre) can be put to the test.

On the whole the FMS stands up well to this scrutiny. Table 3.4 shows that the 1970 census gave a figure of 5·66 smd per acre for the whole of agriculture in England and Wales (excluding horticultural specialist holdings and part-time holdings, as no data for such holdings were included in the FMS tape mentioned on p. 4). When the size-groups are weighted in the correct national proportions, the FMS sample gave a figure of 5·54 smd per acre — a difference of only 2 per cent. The comparison was also reasonably close within each size-group, except that the largest farm businesses in the FMS (4,200 smd and over) appear to be rather less intensive than those farms at the upper end of the scale in the population as a whole.

Table 3.4

Comparison of FMS data and Census data in the
average intensity of production (crops and livestock) in
each size-group, England and Wales, 1970/71[1]

Size-group (smd)	Census weight (per cent)	Census 1970	FMS 1970/71
		(smd per acre)	
275–599	18·7	5·18	4·95[2]
600–1,199	29·5	5·36	5·18
1,200–1,799	15·9	5·44	5·40
1,800–2,399	8·8	5·42	5·56
2,400–4,199	12·6	5·80	5·78
4,200 and over	14·5	7·88	6·94
Weighted average		5·66	5·54

[1] Excluding horticultural specialist holdings and part-time holdings of less than 275 smd.
[2] Based on farms of 300–599 smd, i.e. those of 275–299 smd, comprising about 1 per cent of the sample but not separately tabulated, were assumed to have the same intensity as those of 300–399.

The FMS sample also faithfully reflects a clearly perceptible feature of the population as a whole, namely that the larger the size of business, the greater the average intensity of production per acre.

Having examined this evidence of the representativeness of the FMS in at least one important agricultural characteristic, we may now consider

Table 3.5

Estimated total value of output, input, net income and tenant's capital by size-groups, England and Wales, 1970/71[1]

| | Census data, 1970 | | | Estimates based on FMS 1970/71 (£ million) | | | | | | | |
Size-group (smd)	Holdings ('000)	Smd (mn)	Crops and grass (mn acres)	Gross output	Input Labour[2]	Input Other	Input Total[2]	Farmer's and wife's labour[2]	Net farm income[3]	Management and investment income[4]	Tenant's capital[5]
275–599	51·0	21·7	4·19	256	66	169	235	42	62	20	180
600–1,199	40·8	34·3	6·40	423	85	272	357	33	100	67	284
1,200–1,799	12·8	18·5	3·40	238	44	151	195	9	53	44	147
1,800–2,399	5·0	10·2	1·89	131	25	84	109	3	24	21	80
2,400–4,199	4·8	14·7	2·53	196	36	126	162	2	36	34	110
4,200 and over	2·2	16·8	2·13	199	41	128	169	1	31	30	109
Total	116·6	116·2	20·54	1,443	297	930	1,227	90	306	216	910

1 Excluding specialist horticultural holdings and part-time holdings of less than 275 smd. These two groups had a total of 31·3 mn. smd, i.e. 21 per cent of the England and Wales total for *all* holdings, 147·5 mn. The separate figures were: horticultural specialists 21·4 mn., part-time holdings 9·9 mn.

2 Including farmer's and wife's labour.

3 Gross output less all inputs except farmer's and wife's labour.

4 Net farm income less farmer's and wife's labour.

5 Average of opening and closing valuations.

Table 3.6

Estimated percentage distribution of output, input, net income and tenant's capital by size-groups (smd), England and Wales, 1970/71[1]

Size-group (smd)	Average efficiency ratio	Holdings	Smd	Crops and grass acres	Gross output	Total input[2]	Total labour[2]	Net farm income[3]	Management and investment income[4]	Tenant's capital[5]
275–599	108·8	43·7	18·7	20·4	17·7	19·2	22·1	20·3	9·7	19·8
600–1,199	118·6	35·0	29·5	31·2	29·4	29·0	28·8	32·6	30·6	31·2
1,200–1,799	122·7	11·0	15·9	16·6	16·4	15·9	14·7	17·4	19·9	16·2
1,800–2,399	120·8	4·3	8·8	9·2	9·1	8·9	8·4	7·8	10·2	8·8
2,400–4,199	121·8	4·3	12·6	12·3	13·6	13·2	12·3	11·8	15·7	12·1
4,200 and over	118·4	1·7	14·5	10·4	13·8	13·8	13·7	10·1	13·9	12·0
Total	118·0	100	100	100	100	100	100	100	100	100

For notes, see Table 3.5.

the results of applying FMS output and input data on the 'national' scale. Tables 3.5, 3.6 and 3.7 give these estimates and some derived percentages and ratios by size-groups on an smd basis, while Table 3.8 gives somewhat more limited information on an acreage basis.

Table 3.6 shows that the farms in the smallest size-group (275–599 smd) dispose of 19 per cent of all agricultural inputs in England and Wales and earn about 20 per cent of the net farm income; but because more than half of this net income constitutes the wages of the farmer and wife, these farms earn only just under 10 per cent of the total management and investment income (defined as net income minus farmer's and wife's labour). This residual income is shown in Table 3.7 to represent a return of only 11 per cent on tenant's capital, compared with returns of well over 20 per cent in all the other size-groups and of over 30 per cent in the group of 2,400–4,199 smd.

Table 3.8 indicates a similar situation on the small-acreage farms (many of which are, of course, the same farms as appear in the small smd group). Farms of under 100 acres only earn about half the average rate of return on management and investment obtained on larger farms.

Table 3.7
Some partial productivity ratios, by size of business,
England and Wales, 1970–71

Size-group (smd)	Gross output per acre £	Gross output per £ tenant's capital	Gross output per £ labour[1]	Gross output per smd	Net value added per £ labour[2]	Management and investment income as per cent of tenant's capital
275–599	61	1·42	3·88	11·8	1·30	11·1
600–1,199	66	1·49	4·98	12·3	1·79	23·6
1,200–1,799	70	1·62	5·41	12·9	2·00	29·9
1,800–2,399	69	1·64	5·24	12·8	1·84	26·2
2,400–4,199	77	1·78	5·44	13·3	1·94	30·9
4,200 and over	93	1·83	4·85	11·8	1·73	27·5
Total	70	1·59	4·86	12·4	1·73	23·7

[1] Including farmer's and wife's labour.
[2] Gross output less all inputs except labour, divided by total labour cost including farmer's and wife's labour.

Table 3.8

Estimated percentage distribution of output, input, net income and tenant's capital by size-groups (acres, crops and grass), England and Wales, 1970/71

Size-group (acres, crops and grass)	Average efficiency ratio	Holdings	Crops and grass acres	Gross output	Total input	Net farm income	Management and investment income	Tenant's capital	Management and investment income as per cent of tenant's capital
Under 100	107·3	42·4	13·2	18·4	20·0	19·9	8·9	17·7	12·2
100—	116·6	18·9	13·2	14·7	14·6	16·3	15·2	14·6	23·9
150—	119·4	24·4	28·8	29·1	28·9	28·5	30·4	30·4	23·2
300—	122·9	8·8	19·0	16·9	16·4	16·3	20·1	16·7	27·8
500—	123·7	4·4	16·7	13·8	13·2	12·8	17·0	13·6	29·2
1,000 and over	116·8	1·0	9·1	7·2	6·9	6·1	8·5	7·0	28·2
Total	118·6	100	100	100	100	100	100	100	23·3

The significance to national output of raising the efficiency of the smaller farms

The numerical importance of the small farmers, together with their apparently low efficiency, might lead one to suppose that very substantial gains to the national agricultural output and net farm income could be obtained if the gap between the efficiency of the small farms and the average efficiency of the rest could be remedied. Any move in that direction would, of course, be welcome as it would raise the incomes of the farmers in question, and, at the same time, make better use of national resources. The following calculations, which look first at the possible gain to the profitability of the small farms (which are certainly considerable) and then at the implications for the national agricultural economy, may help to keep the matter in perspective.

If, by increasing their output per unit of input, the 51,000 farms in the smallest smd size-group had been able to attain the average efficiency ratio (output per £100 total input) recorded for all farms of 600 smd and over (120·1) instead of their own low average of 108·8, it can be inferred from Table 3.6 that they would have had a gross output worth £282 million instead of £256 million, giving them an extra £26 million. This would have more than doubled their management and investment income (making it £46 million instead of £20 million) and given them a return on capital of over 25 per cent instead of 11 per cent as recorded. Alternatively, it can be calculated that if they had raised their average efficiency ratio to the same figure of 120·1 referred to above, not by increasing output but by producing the same output with reduced inputs, this would have represented a saving in inputs of £22 million.

The corresponding figures for the 49,500 small-acreage farms (of under 100 acres) show that, by achieving the average efficiency ratio of the rest (120·3), they could have increased their output by some £32 million, or saved £27 million on inputs, and earned a return in the region of 30 per cent on tenant's capital.

These very hypothetical gains would evidently be sufficient to transform the financial situation of the small farms in question, and, from their point of view, it is clear that any steps which could be taken to bring them to a more normal output/input ratio, whether by raising yields, intensifying systems or finding alternative and more productive employment for the farmer during part of his time, would be of great value — at least in monetary terms. A rather different perspective, however, is obtained if it is recognised that even the substantial hypothetical improvements postulated here (say, £26 million in 1970–71 conditions) on the arbitrary assumption that the handicapped group could be raised to the level of the rest, would represent an increase of only about 2 per cent in *total* agricultural output (or a saving of 2 per cent in inputs); total net farm income would be raised by about 8½ per cent and the average return to management and investment as a percentage of tenant's capital would rise from 24 per cent to 27 per cent.

Thus it must be broadly concluded that because the diseconomies of small size, which are examined in more detail in Chapter 5, are now apparently confined to a relatively small section of British agriculture (about 20 per cent), their removal, while being of great benefit to the 50,000 farmers concerned, would not very substantially affect the national agricultural economy as a whole.

Notes

[1] MAFF, *Farm Classification in England and Wales 1973*, p. 1.

[2] Farm Management Survey data show that smd's bear a much closer relationship to gross output and to the value of tenant's capital than does acreage. When the 2,400 farms recorded in 1971/72 were classified by 17 acreage size-groups and 19 smd size-groups respectively, the variation between groups in gross output per acre was greater than in gross output per smd (coefficients of variation of 21·4 per cent and 5·4 per cent respectively). For closing valuations (tenant's capital) the coefficients were 21·2 per cent and 7·2 per cent respectively.

[3] MAFF, *Farm Classification in England and Wales 1971. See also* Ashton, J., and Cracknell, B.E., 'Agricultural Holdings and Farm Business Structure in England and Wales' *Journ. Ag. Econs,* vol. XIV, no. 4, 1961.

[4] Harrison, A., *The financial structure of farm businesses,* Univ. of Reading, Dept of Ag. Econs. and Management, 1972.

[5] A summary and discussion will be found in Edwards, Angela, and Rogers, A. (eds), *Agricultural Resources,* Faber 1974, chapter 2.

[6] See Ball, A.G., and Heady, E.O. (eds), *Size, Structure and Future of Farms,* Iowa Univ. Press, 1972, p. 96 where some further references are given.

[7] Shepherd, G.S., *Farm Policy : New Directions,* Iowa State Univ. Press, 1964, p. 93.

[8] The reader should bear in mind that the numbers in the various size-groups have been affected to some extent by 'statistical' amalgamation as well as by real amalgamation; see p. 24.

4 The Meaning of Efficiency

The term 'efficiency' has already been used on a number of occasions in the preceding chapters, but it must be recognised that it is subject to a variety of interpretations. To a farmer, it might imply the achievement of a high output from his land; alternatively, 'being efficient' might mean generating high levels of business profit. An observer of the internal structure of the agricultural industry might compare the 'efficiency' achieved by farms of different sizes or types by relating the value of their respective outputs to their respective production costs. Taking a national view, consideration of the 'efficiency' of agriculture would involve somehow measuring how effectively agriculture uses its share of the national resources of manpower, energy, land area and so forth in comparison with other sectors of the economy.

In the present study, agricultural efficiency is taken to be at a maximum when the greatest possible product is achieved from a given stock of resources, or conversely, when a minimum input of resources is used to produce a given level of output. At peak efficiency, it would be impossible to achieve a higher level of production by redistributing resources of land, capital, labour or management. The extent to which this economy of factor use is achieved can be studied for a single farm or firm but the same concept can also be extended to a study of resource efficiency at the level of the agricultural industry or of the entire national economy.

The principal and also most convenient measure of production used here is the monetary value of agricultural output; that is, physical output (tons of grain, gallons of milk, and so forth) multiplied by their respective prices (including subsidies). However, this is only one of several possible bases; for example, in wartime, a nation might be more concerned with producing the greatest quantity of food energy, and, in such circumstances, calories would be a more appropriate measure.

At the level of the individual farm, the rewards from farming consist partly of monetary income, which is spent primarily on goods and services from other sectors of the economy, and partly of the non-monetary satisfaction derived from business independence, living in a rural environment, social standing and so forth. Moreover, the (alleged) diminishing marginal utility of monetary income and the progressive marginal rates of income

45

tax probably mean that the non-monetary rewards contribute to different extents at different income levels. Hence, while farms are basically treated in this study as 'pure' profit maximisers, their tendency to derive part of their utility from non-monetary sources must not be disregarded. The same might also be said of non-monetary satisfactions enjoyed by the farm workers, the undoubted existence of which probably goes some way to explain the gap in earnings between agricultural workers and other manual workers.[1]

The 'total utility' argument can be applied at all levels of comparison, up to the national or international level. The non-monetary benefits conferred on society (or the costs imposed) by the activities of the agricultural sector should be added to (or subtracted from) farming's monetary contribution to the nation's welfare. These non-monetary elements range from the satisfaction of having an internal food supply and hence less dependence on foreign suppliers, to the stability of behaviour, the sound commonsense, or even the stolidity, which the rural population contributes to the British character. But if the rural population prevents the realisation of potential increases in welfare by impeding social change by adopting an unduly conservative outlook, then this could with some reason be treated as a negative element in agriculture's contribution in a system of full social accounting.

Private and social costs

Given that farming can not only bestow non-monetary benefits on society but can also impose non-monetary costs, it is perhaps appropriate to point out that farming's use of resources is dictated primarily by private as opposed to total costs. A farmer will make his decision on how much herbicide to use principally by balancing its cost to him against the benefits it can give in terms of higher crop yields; it will be of secondary consideration *to him* that this herbicide may enter the river system and necessitate the use of an alternative and more costly water-source for industrial and domestic purposes. These 'external' costs of using the chemical should be added to the 'private' costs borne by the farmer. While it is true that the more irresponsible misuses of resources liable to impose costs on other forms of production or on society as a whole can be, and are, legislated against, the preparation and enforcement of this legislation itself must be regarded as a cost, although it is probably the less expensive alternative.

The ease with which external and private costs can be added to give a

46

level of total production costs, which will in turn be reflected in product price, will depend on the seriousness of the external cost and the ease with which its source can be identified. Thus, while the sources of diesel fumes from tractor exhausts are easily identified, they have little effect on society as a whole because of the open environments in which tractors work. It must be assumed that society decides that the cost of exhaust suppression, involving the necessity of legislation and higher product prices, is greater than the benefits so gained. (This does not necessarily mean that society is right, and individual tractor drivers might well disagree with society's judgements.) On the other hand, many would argue that changes in farming techniques have resulted in a serious deterioration in the scenic beauty of the countryside, but the causes of this deterioration − for example the technical advances manifested by large-scale field machinery − are difficult to identify precisely; furthermore, the relatively weak feeling of deprivation experienced by the casual visitor is difficult to dragoon into combat against the clear private-cost benefits which the farming community can muster in favour of such 'advances'. Perhaps external costs are most likely to be recovered from their originators where the victim is another producer; if a fish hatchery is damaged by river pollution from silage effluent, it is in the hatchery proprietor's interests to extract damages from the careless farmer.

Where society in general is the victim of an external cost, such as occurs as the result of urban sprawl, but where separate individuals are not acutely affected, the imposition of compensatory transfer payments from the perpetrators to the losers is unlikely to be implemented. Although society attempts to impose the 'external' costs of agriculture onto its private costs by such means as control of the use of dangerous chemicals, control of water pollution and limited planning control over the erection of farm buildings, the imposition is only partial. No surety can be afforded to the hypothesis that the most 'efficient' scales of farming as indicated by the value of production in relation to the costs of production (where both are measured at market prices) are those which most improve the welfare either of the individual farmer or of society in general because large-scale, more 'efficient' farming may impose social costs which are not incurred in smaller-scale units; for example, large-scale pig production *may* cause problems of smell and noise which do not arise with smaller production units. All that can be said about levels of efficiency by reference to the monetary values of output and the costs of inputs is that performances can be ranked only according to those elements which are specifically recognised and measured as output and inputs − and this means basically 'private' benefits and costs. This being so, any adjustments made to the structure of agriculture in an attempt to increase the efficiency of the industry as a whole should be wary of neglecting the effect upon those intangible benefits or costs of production which, though they have no place in the farm accounts, have a very real meaning for the community as a whole.

Distortions of the price mechanism

Measures of efficiency which look at the value of output and the costs of inputs can also be distorted by the various mechanisms which determine prices. In a state of 'perfect' competition (where there are so many buyers and sellers of goods that one individual cannot account for a significant proportion of the total and thereby influence the market price, and where there is no state interference in the market) prices of goods will reflect the quantity and quality of factors entering into their production. The price mechanism, if factors of production are free to be switched between lines of production and between firms, will ensure that consumer desires are reflected in what is produced. However, the state may modify this pattern if it considers that the expressed demands of private consumers fail to take sufficient account of the welfare of the community as a whole or of certain sections of it. If, for example, it is considered socially desirable and politically possible to narrow the income gap between the rich and the poor, an income transfer from rich to poor can be effected by a subsidy financed from progressive taxation. This will permit some reduction in the market prices of foods relative to the prices of other goods. This distorts the free market price system. An income transfer in the opposite direction could be effected by a tax on food, which would increase its market price.

Therefore, whenever efficiency is measured by the relationship between the value of outputs and the cost of inputs, great caution must be exercised in comparing efficiencies between industries where there are varying extents of governmental involvement in the mechanism of price formation (including the role of government in regulating international trade), or where the degree of competition differs.

Even comparisons of efficiency between agricultural sectors on the basis of current values of output and costs are hazardous. If, at a price review, the government increases the price received for milk while leaving that of cereals unchanged, then the apparent efficiency of the milk industry will take a sudden jump upwards. An opposite effect might be achieved by placing a subsidy on fertilizer costs, to the benefit of cereal farmers.

It would seem safest to restrict comparisons of efficiency to farms of the same type[2] so that the effects of price or cost distortions are minimised, and in our analysis of the available data we have tried to keep this constantly in mind. Even then, one must be careful to compare like with like. The large farm, which perhaps uses proportionally greater quantities of 'artificial' fertilizer, may appear from an input/output calculation to be more efficient than it really is, because it receives a subsidy on fertilizer. If the value of the subsidy were added back in to show the 'true' cost of fertilizer, the larger farm might be no more efficient than the smaller: this is the view which the nation as a whole might be expected to take when using measures of efficiency as a guide in its allocation of national resources. If a proposal were made to redistribute resources between farms in order to increase the agricultural product, it would be foolish to base such a redistribution on performances calculated on factor prices which did not reflect actual factor scarcity, or on product prices which did not accurately reflect the quantity and quality of factors entering into their production.

Imputed costs

The problem of possible price distortion is felt in its most acute form when the cost of inputs has to be imputed because no cash payment is involved. The most prominent items of this kind are imputed rents for owner-occupied land and the value to be attached to the farmer's personal contribution to production. No annual direct payments are made by farm businesses for the use of owner-occupied land or for the work of the farmer, yet both represent part of the national resources used by farming and hence must be accounted for when assessing the efficiency of the industry, or when drawing comparisons between any of its sectors. Any study of the relative efficiency of different sizes of farm business must therefore impute values for these two factors of production.

If we could be confident that the inputs for which imputed costs were used did not contribute in any major way to the results which indicate that large businesses are more efficient, the absolute level of costs ascribed to them would be relatively unimportant. For example, if the input of land were to be measured by some notional rent figure, and if this rent increased in direct proportion with the size of business (leaving aside the question of how size might be measured) then the imputed rent figure would not affect the efficiency ranking of different sizes of business; this ranking would be attributable to other inputs. However, the labour input of the farmer (as measured by hours of manual labour) obviously cannot increase indefinitely with size of business, and once a certain point of full employment is reached, his labour becomes a fixed cost which is 'spread' over an increasing volume of production. In this case, the level of cost imputed to the farmer can, and (as we will show later) does, have a profound influence on the result derived from measuring the comparative overall efficiency of small and large businesses.

The two principal methods of arriving at imputed costs are: (1) to look at what is paid to similar factors of production in similar occupations but where actual payments are made; or (which is not quite the same) (2) to consider what the inputs in question could earn in their best-paid alternative employment – their 'transfer earnings or opportunity costs'. Rental values for owner-occupied land can be imputed using the first method by reference to tenanted land for which annual rents are paid in farms of a similar size and type. It must be admitted that the mechanism by which these rents are themselves determined and changed does not perfectly and solely reflect the contribution to production which the land is capable of making during the period to which the rents relate. This point is forcibly brought home whenever MAFF publishes statistics comparing the *average* rents currently being paid for existing tenancies with *new* rents negotiated in new tenancy agreements. Moreover, the practice of treating all farms as tenanted when making comparisons of farm income of efficiency is open to criticism now that more than half the holdings in England and Wales are owner-occupied. However, the alternative of imputing a land charge based on some percentage of the market value of land is open to even more objections, a major one being that land values are the product of many influences besides the annual agricultural income which the land is thought to be capable of yielding in the future. However, although we believe that this question deserves further investigation, it appears (see Chapter 6), in practice, that the relative constancy of the physical input of land and buildings per £100 of gross output in different sizes of business and the smallness of the rent figure in relation to present-day total British agricultural costs combine to make the overall output/input measure of efficiency rather insensitive to the level of imputed rents which is chosen for owner-occupiers. Even if the imputed rents are biased in one direction or the other, we see no reason to suppose that the bias is materially different between different sizes of business.

A rather different situation arises with regard to the imputed cost of the work of the farmer and his wife. For purposes of economic analysis, their physical labour is usually charged in the farm accounts at the hourly rate paid to farm workers, but this is only a partial calculation because the farmer also contributes managerial effort which, at least in the larger farm businesses, must reflect a level of ability that could command high salaries in other industries.[3] On the other hand, estimating what farmers *could* earn in other occupations and charging those salaries to the farm business increases the arbitrary element in measuring efficiency. Each farmer would need to be assessed individually and there is no guarantee that if the farmer took a job elsewhere he could in all cases earn as much as a farm worker, at least in the short term. Also the non-monetary elements of income (independence, job satisfaction, housing, etc.) would have to be taken into account.

Non-equilibrium conditions

The existence of non-equilibrium conditions, that is where farmers have not yet had sufficient time to adjust their production to a changed level of costs or product prices, adds yet a further situation which calls into question the validity of comparisons of efficiency which are based on calculations in monetary terms. A sudden and unexpected rise in the market price of beef will make beef production appear temporarily more 'efficient' than other lines of production which have not received a price boost. It could be expected that, in response to the increased product price, beef producers would, given time, expand production, thereby reducing its temporary high price and would simultaneously increase the demand for their inputs, forcing up the price of calves, feedstuffs, labour and so forth. (This of course assumes that the demand for the product and the supply of factors are less than infinitely elastic with respect to price.) The combined effect of the longer-term product and factor price adjustments could well be to cut back or perhaps even nullify the short-term apparent gain in 'efficiency'.

In the real world, stable equilibrium is seldom achieved in agricultural production. The relative strengths of demand for foods are constantly being modified by the general rise in consumers' incomes; changes in government policy occur in response to changes in the economic, political and social climate; to these must be added changes in supply conditions, such as advances in production techniques which will not necessarily proceed at the same rate in all enterprises, and changes in relative factor costs such as a rise in the world price of animal feedstuffs or of oil which could be expected to impinge more on certain sectors of the UK's agricultural industry than on others. Indeed, the correction of disequilibrium is a vital part of the adjustment mechanism by which, impelled by the difference in rewards, factors are switched from the less efficient systems of production and sizes of business to the more efficient, and any study of size and efficiency cannot ignore such movements. However, a certain degree of confidence in the permanence of the changed relationships will be necessary for factor movement to occur.

The essential point from this discussion of disequilibrium is that, because of the time period involved, price and cost changes brought about by external influences occur *before* changes in factor allocation take place. In judging whether there are lasting differences in efficiency, whether between farms of different sizes or of different types, on the basis of the ratio of the value of production to the level of costs, it would be necessary to distinguish between those efficiency differences which persist because of long-run immobility of factors (a major preoccupation of many studies of the economics of agriculture), those efficiency differences which will prove to be sensitive to the dynamics of the adjustment process and those of a transitory and illusory nature which are caused by temporary fluctuations in prices and costs. For example, in 1971/72, because UK agriculture benefited through a general rise in product prices, and prices of inputs had not yet risen correspondingly, there was a transient improvement in the industry's 'efficiency ratio'. In the ensuing year, when the much higher prices of feed grains and the general rise in the cost of manufactured goods, as well as in wages, had been reflected in farmers' production costs, the level of 'efficiency' could have been expected to drop back towards its previous level. Clearly, to recommend a long-term switching of resources on the basis of apparent type-of-farming differences in efficiency which were in fact attributable to short-term price changes would have been erroneous. Assessments of changes in absolute or relative levels of efficiency thus call for some averaging over time.

The distribution of purchasing power

One further digression into the implications of using current prices and subsidies when calculating output and inputs to assess efficiency is necessary. If, for political reasons, a redistribution of the country's national income is undertaken by, for example, a progressive taxation of high-income families and welfare payments to low-income families, the pattern of overall demand will be shifted, both between food and non-food products, and between different types of food. This will, in turn, change relative prices, so that the optimum, or most 'efficient' pattern of production (in terms of the greatest value of goods obtainable from the nation's productive resources) under one distribution of the nation's income may well *not* be the optimum under an alternative distribution. It is impossible to state objectively which income distribution and hence which production pattern is 'best' for the nation as a whole, because any redistribution involves making some people better off and some worse off. No acceptable unit of 'satisfaction' yet exists by which satisfaction lost can be subtracted from satisfaction gained to produce an aggregate net gain or loss. Hence in our study of efficiency, as measured using market prices, we must be content to accept the country's income distribution as given.

While measurements of efficiency in terms of the value of output in relation to the cost of the factors required for its production, with both product and factor prices taken from the market, are open to criticism, such measurements remain the most accessible and the most useful. The classic argument in support of any knowledge which is less than complete can be called upon to justify their use; imperfect measurement of efficiency is better than no measurement, as long as we are aware of the deficiencies in our yardsticks. However, conclusions or recommendations based on the findings from imperfect measurements must always carry caveats.

The problem in hand

In studying the relationship between farm size and efficiency, we are not directly concerned with comparing the efficiency of resource use in agriculture and other industries, although a more efficient re-allocation of resources within agriculture would have repercussions on the best inter-industry balance. Nor are we considering the relative efficiency of the various enterprises making up a farm business, although, again, mis-allocation at the enterprise level will be reflected in the performance of the farm as a whole. The main area of study here is the economic performance achieved by farms of different sizes and the implications which variations in performance might hold for the re-allocation of resources between size-groups in pursuit of greater overall efficiency of the farming industry. In explaining differences in the efficiency of farms, it will be necessary to probe into their use of resources to show the close links existing between the performances obtained from resources (particularly labour) on individual farms and the efficient allocation of resources between farms of different sizes. Hence we are really looking at three closely related questions: (1) do farms of different sizes use their resources with differing degrees of efficiency? (2) can poor performances be linked to a poor allocation of resources *within* farms, that is, is the organisation at farm level as efficient as possible? and (3) would a reallocation of resources between farms of different sizes improve the efficiency of the industry as a whole? (A fuller consideration of the conditions of efficiency is given in an appendix to this chapter.)

The types of data available for 'efficiency' measures

The ratios derived from farm business accounts which are commonly used to enable comparisons to be drawn between the levels of efficiency of different farms or groups of farms include the following: value of output (gross or net) per acre, value of output (gross or net) per man, value of output per £100 worth of inputs (or its reciprocal, the total cost of producing £100 worth of output) and value of output per £100 labour. These are all measures of *average* performance, or average value products (AVP), and give no direct indication of marginal efficiency, that is, of what happens to the value of output when *extra* or *fewer* units of resource are used. For example, while output per man on a five-man farm may be £5,000, there is no guarantee that, by engaging a sixth man, output will increase by a further £5,000. Indeed, the extra man might be forced to spend most of his time standing around idle because there was already sufficient labour to work the farm machinery, and so might contribute little towards expanding output. The last unit of any factor employed (in this case the sixth man) is termed the 'marginal' unit and the increase in the value of output, which results from engaging the 'marginal' unit of the factor, is termed its marginal value product (MVP). It is the performance of 'marginal' units, not average performance, which is important to any study of improving efficiency by the re-allocation of resources.

In our example, if the marginal value product of the sixth man was £3,000, we would need to know how much the farm from which he transferred had suffered in terms of output by his leaving before we could judge whether his transfer had resulted in an overall increase in output (or improvement in efficiency) of the agricultural industry. Hence, before suggesting any re-allocation of resources between farms of different sizes, it would be necessary to identify those farms where marginal value products of resources, whether land, labour, capital or management, are low, and those where MVP's are high. Switching resources from the first to the second group would result in the resources being employed in a more efficient way — that is, in producing a greater value of output. This process would cause MVP's to converge, and the most efficient resource allocation will be achieved when output cannot be increased by any further re-allocation.

Farms as marginal units

When we move from considering the allocation of units of certain resources between farms to considering the allocation of total agricultural production between the numerous farms of various sizes which compose the agricultural industry, then whole farms can be treated as 'marginal' units, representing a bundle of combined resources. If a small farm is amalgamated with another farm to form one larger unit, it is reasonable to take the net gain to the industry by this marginal re-allocation of resources as being the larger amalgamated unit's excess of output over the sum of the outputs from the two independent smaller units, adjusted for any resources (such as labour) which may have been released from farming as a consequence of the amalgamation. In terms of the average performance, measured by the value of output per unit of input (say £100 worth of input) an increase would be expected — in other words there would have been an improvement in efficiency.

Are small farms potential large farms?

There is no guarantee that marginal transfers of resources of the type described above will always result in an improvement in overall efficiency. It is often assumed in discussions of structural adjustment in farming that small farms and large farms experience (or could experience) the same response of output to different quantities of input (that is, they operate in the context of the same production functions) but that larger farms have progressed 'further along' the relationships while the small farms are, for some reason, being held back. If larger farms can show higher efficiency in terms of output per unit of input, then the assumption leads to the conclusion that, once the restraining forces which are acting on the small farms' ability to expand are removed, they are capable of becoming as efficient as the existing larger farms.

However, this assumption is probably not valid in all cases. Farms of the same type but of different sizes may *not* be all on the same production function because of, say, differences in the technical abilities of their operators, climatic differences, and so forth. We may be implying a universal function which is indicated in the diagram below by the dotted line ABC (Figure 4.1), but which, in fact, does not exist from the point of view of the individual farmer, as he may be incapable of moving from A to B or from B to C because of limitations in his own situation and personal capacity. This could be one factor explaining the continued existence of farms of different sizes; perhaps each size is an 'optimum' for a given set of circumstances.

It is quite conceivable that the small, medium and large farms, located on their respective functions at points A, B and C, may be organised by their operators in such a way that each is as efficient as possible — that is, achieving the highest output obtainable given the resources available to the farmer. Among these resources, the farmer will have to accept some as being immutable or 'fixed', at least in the short term. He certainly cannot

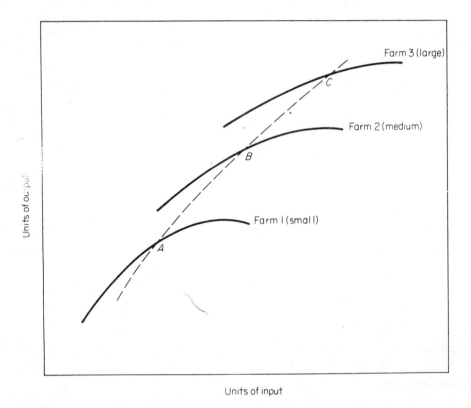

Fig. 4.1   Derivation   of   a   false   production   function   from   inter-farm comparisons

56

change the type of soil with which he is working, except by moving to another farm. He has to accept that his innate management ability and physical capacity for work cannot be altered to correspond more closely to the size of farm on which he happens to be working and may, therefore, be under-used in some cases and stretched beyond reasonable limits in others. This rigidity of factor use is a major obstacle to farming's ability to adapt to changing economic and technical conditions, and if land, labour, capital and management were all instantly transferable between uses and locations, many of the problems of current agricultural policy would evaporate.[4]

A comparison of output/input ratios assumes that, within each size-group of farms, operators would benefit from raising that ratio to a maximum and are aiming to do so, given the constraints on organisational possibilities imposed by 'fixed' resources. However, not all operators pursue this goal, at least in terms of the monetary values of output receipts and input expenses. They may follow an indeterminate but equally tenable concept of 'good husbandry', which would involve conserving the long-term productive capacity of the land and establishing a pattern of resource use which would not place undue reliance on the continuing availability of 'external' supplies. Different goals *could* explain different levels of performance between large and small farms, as also could differences in the awareness of the physical performances that are attainable — that is, greater degree of failure on the part of the smaller farmers to move to the best point on the production function which defines their possibilities.

To summarise, while data on average levels of performance achieved by farms of different size are available, we cannot necessarily suppose that (1) these performances are the result of farms being organised in the most efficient way in each size-group within the constraints imposed by the fixity of certain resources — notably land and the farmer himself — although it seems likely that the tendency is always in that direction; (2) the performances currently achieved by larger businesses can be reached by encouraging present small businesses to grow in size, although later we shall suggest that such levels are probably attainable. We shall show that the greatest single source of inefficiency (low output/input ratio) on the small farm is the relatively ineffectual use of the farmer's own labour; but amalgamating holdings to counteract this imbalance raises the questions of the ability of a sufficient number of the present farmers to cope with the greater demands on management and the situation of the farmers who would be made redundant by the amalgamation.

Prima facie evidence about marginal products from factor movements

So far, the possible re-allocation of resources between farms of different sizes has been discussed as if it could be brought about in conformity to some great central plan. But, in the UK, central planning is not behind most factor movements; factors move largely because of differences in the rewards attainable. Workers tend to shift to those jobs in which net benefits, both monetary and non-monetary, are highest. Capital is channelled into investments according to the interest which can be earned, suitably discounted for risk.

Differences in the rewards attainable by a factor in different employments may exist because the marginal productivities of the factor vary. For example, if a farmer employing six men calculated that a seventh man could boost production (net of any other additional costs) by £1,000 (so that the marginal value product[5] of the seventh man is £1,000) then this farmer would be willing to offer a man up to £1,000 to attract him. If another farmer could offer the same man only £700 (because his net marginal value product to him would be only £700), then the first farmer will offer the more attractive wage and, non-monetary benefits being equal, the first farmer will get his man. In other words, because the marginal products of factors differ, payments to factors differ, and hence factors tend to flow from those farms where they have low marginal productivities to farms where they have high marginal productivities. This redistribution, achieved through the price system and factor mobility, is exactly the sort of thing which a central planner would want to achieve, although, for him to do so, he would need much data on marginal performances of factors.

It will be shown elsewhere that those farms which have been most rapidly declining in numbers — that is, the smallest farms — are also those which tend to have low performances, measured in output per £100 input. Both declining numbers and low average products could be explained by the low marginal products of factors, and this double association is probably sufficient to establish the general existence of low marginal factor productivities on farms in these categories, although this of course does not constitute a proof.

Summary of the consideration of the meaning of 'efficiency'

An 'efficient' farm is one which maximises the output it achieves from its available resources, including its management. While part of the

58

agricultural product cannot be measured quantitatively, monetary values are a convenient yardstick by which most of the industry's heterogeneous output can be reduced to a common denominator. The achieving of maximum efficiency is essentially a process of scrutinising marginal relationships and appropriately re-allocating resources to maximise output. This applies as much to the 'efficient' allocation of factors between different sizes of farms and to adjustment between agriculture and other industries as it does to factor use in a particular farm enterprise, such as milk production. Unfortunately, data on marginal factor performances are not widely available — but data on average performances are. However, it is possible — if only as an approximation — to infer levels of marginal performance of resources between different size-groups of farm from average data, and hence suggest the direction in which resources should be redirected to increase overall efficiency, as long as care is taken not to overlook the assumptions which, as has been indicated, are implied in such a procedure.

Appendix: the condition of efficiency

The principle of equimarginal returns can be drawn upon to indicate the most efficient allocation of resources. This principle can be applied to allocate resources between enterprises within a farm business, between farms, between type and size-groups of farms, and, finally, even between agriculture and other industries. Within this framework, resources are allocated most efficiently when the following conditions hold true:

1 Resources must be allocated within each farm in such a manner that the increment in the value of total output caused by using the last unit of resource (termed that resource's marginal value product or MVP) must be the same in each of the resource's uses. For example, a worker should not be used to step up output on a cereals enterprise if he could increase output by a greater value in a dairy enterprise. If a farmer is thinking of buying £1,000 worth of machinery, he should buy extra barn equipment rather than other types only if, after allowing for the working life of the equipment, that additional capital increases the value of output more than any other type of machinery. Such a process of allocating resources according to marginal value products will tend to make the marginal value products equal in each use because of the Law of Diminishing Returns. This may be summarised by saying that, with other resources remaining unchanged, the greater the quantity of a resource already in use, the smaller will be the additional output attained by using one more unit of that resource. Hence, using more of a resource which was originally little used will lower its marginal value product, and using less of a resource originally greatly used will raise its marginal value product. Where the marginal value products of, say, labour differ on one farm between the cereal and dairy enterprises, being greater in dairying, they can be equated by switching labour from cereals to dairying, and at the same time an increase in the *total* value of the farm's output will occur.

2 Resources must be distributed between farms so that marginal value products are equal. For example, if manpower or land has lower MVP on small farms than on large ones, the national average cost of producing a unit of output could be reduced by a process of transferring manpower or land from the small to the large farms. This process of adjustment would increase the efficiency of agriculture, although it must be remembered that this may also involve costs and benefits, mainly of a social kind, which are not measured by the price system upon which efficiency measures are based.

3 Resources must be distributed between farming types and geographical

regions so that MVPs are equated.

4   The various factors of production must be allocated between industries (among which agriculture is but one) to bring about equal MVP's between industries.

5   Resources must be allocated so that their value products, discounted over time, are equal. This last condition recognises that an allocation which yields £x in the immediate future is preferable to one which yields £x in the more distant future; the problem of choosing which re-allocation of resources would maximise the current value of a future stream of earnings is too complex to be considered here.

If national resources are allocated according to the above conditions, then it may be supposed that the greatest possible value of product is being derived from them — that is, they are being used in the most efficient way.

Notes

[1] See Bellerby, J.R. *Agriculture and Industry: Relative Income* Macmillan, London 1956.

[2] This point is strongly expressed in Raeburn, J.R. 'Economies of Scale in Farming', *Journal of Agricultural Economics 13,* June 1958, pp. 72–9.

[3] For some discussion of this point, see Britton, D.K., 'The analysis of net farm income: an examination of Farm Management Survey data', *Journal of Agricultural Economics* vol. XXI, no. 3, 1970.

[4] For further discussion of the implied but non-existent general production function see Heady, E.O., *Economics of agricultural production and resource use,* Prentice-Hall, 1952, pp. 310–11.

[5] The term *net* marginal value product allows for any additional costs incurred (other than that of the factor under consideration). For example, the seventh man may generate an extra £1,200 of output (marginal value product), but, to enable him to work, the farmer may be involved in buying extra machinery which costs £200 per year.

5 Recent Evidence on Size and Efficiency

There are few sources of evidence about size and efficiency in British agriculture which are nation-wide in scope. The Zuckerman report on *Scale of Enterprise in Farming,* mentioned in Chapter 1, related to the mid-1950s. Although, being based on the MAFF's Farm Management Survey, it referred to the whole of England and Wales, its conclusions may not necessarily apply in the changed conditions of the early 1970s. A more recent study of farm productivity made by the Economic Development Committee for Agriculture in 1973 and quoted on p. 11 showed that, among the 133 farms included in the survey, those classed as highly productive (on the basis of output/input ratios over a three-year period) were of an average size of 290 acres (including rough grazings adjusted to their crops-and-grass equivalent acreage), while those classed as being of low productivity were of an average size of 159 acres, This difference was tested statistically and was found to be significant in spite of the small size of the sample. The data used came from the same source as those which are analysed annually in the MAFF report on *Farm Incomes in England and Wales* – that is, the Farm Management Survey (FMS) – and more details of the relationship, as well as figures for more recent years, can be found in that series of MAFF publications.

Further evidence could, no doubt, be obtained from the data collected annually by the National Farmers Union in its *Farm Accounts Scheme,* but we are not aware of any published analysis of those data that is specifically directed to the size/efficiency relationship.

We therefore found no alternative but to come back to the FMS data, and, in any case, if any worthwhile comparison was to be made with the findings of the Zuckerman report of 1961, the FMS data would be the appropriate source since the survey in the mid-1950s had formed the basis of that report.

The FMS is a yearly analysis of the accounts of some 2,500 farms that are collected by university agricultural economists in all parts of England and Wales under an arrangement with MAFF. The farmers are anonymous as far as MAFF is concerned, and they provide the information entirely voluntarily and in co-operation with the universities' field recording staffs on a confidential basis. The primary purpose of the FMS, which has been continued annually without interruption since 1937, is not that of this study (to examine the relationship between size and efficiency) but to provide measures of year-to-year changes in receipts, expenses and net income on different types and sizes of farms. The use of the data for purposes other than those for which the FMS was intended presented difficulties to the Zuckerman Committee and these difficulties still largely apply. Nevertheless, such a comprehensive, long-established and continuing source of data could not fail to provide very useful material for our purpose.

The Zuckerman report used acreage as the principal measure of farm size, expressing the area of rough grazings belonging to any individual farm — as opposed to communal grazing — in terms of its value as average pasture, where appropriate.

Unfortunately for purposes of comparison, since 1965, MAFF has largely abandoned acreage as a basis of size classification when analysing FMS data, and has adopted instead a classification based on standard man-days, as described in Chapter 3. This change is quite defensible on the grounds that as a measure of size, smd's reflect both the physical size of the farm and the intensity with which the area is used. They also facilitate comparisons between farms of different types but of similar business size, in that they help to overcome the kind of difficulty that would arise if a small but intensive dairy farm were ranked lower in size than a larger arable farm purely on account of their respective acreages; such a procedure would not properly reflect their relative size in terms of turnover or any of the other yardsticks commonly used to measure size of business.

The Zuckerman Committee was careful not to draw inappropriate comparisons between farms of similar acreage but of different types, and its conclusions were based on a classification of farms into type-groups, within which acreage *did* give a reasonable measure of relative business size. Farms were classified as dairy, livestock, arable or mixed, according to the commodity or commodities which accounted for most of the output. It should be noted that this type-of-farming classification differs from that currently used by the MAFF which is based on the relative labour requirements of different enterprises.

The Zuckerman Committee did not consider certain 'specialist' types of farm such as poultry farms and horticultural businesses. In retrospect, this was perhaps an important omission, in view of the growth of large-scale egg and poultry production, and of the particular nature and circumstances of the horticultural industry.

Although the MAFF reports of the FMS now make little use of acreage classification, we were able to go back to the original data and make certain analyses in acreage size-groups which enable us to make some degree of comparison with the Zuckerman report. At the same time, we were able to extend the analysis on an smd basis of classification in a more detailed way than is given in the annual published tables. The year for which we made these special analyses was 1970/71, and this explains why that year is mentioned so frequently in these pages, even though more recent data are now available in the usual form.

In this chapter we look at efficiency (represented by value of gross output per £100 total inputs) first in relation to size as measured in acres and then in relation to size as measured in smd.

Table 5.1

Average efficiency ratio on farms of different sizes
and by type of farm, England and Wales, 1970/71

Size-group (acres, crops and grass)	Average acreage (all types of farm)	Number of farms	Efficiency ratio (output/input x 100)				
			All types	Dairy	Livestock (cattle and sheep)	Cropping	Mixed
20—	37	178	99·9	103·8	92·1	105·5	(—)
50—	74	494	108·9	111·7	102·3	108·8	106·9
100—	123	416	116·6	118·0	116·6	116·4	111·1
150—	173	319	117·3	117·7	118·5	116·3	117·7
200—	223	238	120·3	118·9	120·6	123·3	117·9
250—	274	184	122·1	120·6	125·7	120·4	123·4
300—	345	225	122·8	118·4	126·4	126·2	119·0
400—	443	148	123·0	118·2	131·7	125·1	116·9
500—	540	96	123·2	122·5	118·6	124·9	124·2
600—	647	55	121·4	121·7	(—)	120·4	(—)
700—	747	29	121·9	(123·4)	(—)	126·7	(—)
800—	900	44	124·2	(120·2)	(—)	126·3	(—)
1,000—	1,057	12	125·8	(—)	(—)	(—)	(—)
1,200—	(1,294)	6	(117·0)	(—)	(—)	(—)	(—)
1,500 and over	1,844	12	117·3	(—)	(—)	(—)	(—)

Figures in brackets indicate that less than ten farms were recorded in the group.

Size (in acres) and efficiency

The farm accounts collected in England and Wales in 1970/71 showed that the efficiency ratio increased from the lowest acreage groups to the highest. The increase was most marked in the transition from 20 to 150 acres; it was still quite perceptible between 150 and 400 acres; but beyond 400 acres there was no further consistent upward movement, nor were there sufficient numbers of farm accounts in the groups beyond 700 acres to give any very reliable measurement. The figures are given in Table 5.1 and in Figure 5.1.

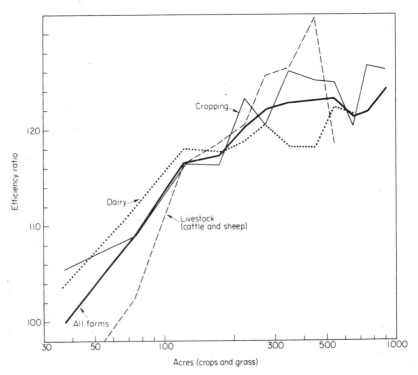

Fig. 5.1   Average efficiency ratio by size and type of farm, England and Wales, 1970/71

The low level of the efficiency ratio on farms of less than 100 acres is to be seen in all of the main types of farming. It has to be remembered, however, that at any level of farm-size within each type efficiency varies considerably between farms, and the data emphatically do *not* show that

66

all large farms are more efficient than all small farms. The table and graph are to be read as indicating the general tendency which, in spite of inter-farm variation, emerges quite clearly. The extent of inter-farm variation within size-groups is examined more closely in a later section dealing with size of business (smd).

In the first and second acreage size-groups (up to 100 acres), the live-stock farms (rearing cattle and/or sheep) appear to be considerably less efficient than other types of farm. This is partly, no doubt, a reflection of the lower intensity per acre on the livestock farms, They had an average gross output of only £50 per acre in the 50—100 acres group, compared with £77 per acre on cropping farms and £102 per acre on dairy farms. However, in the larger size-groups (above 150 acres), the low output per acre on livestock farms is matched by correspondingly low total inputs, and the efficiency ratio compares well with other types of farming. It would appear that the imputed cost of farmer's and wife's labour as an element in the cost structure has a particularly strong influence on the low efficiency ratio of small livestock farms.

Size-group 50—100 acres	Dairy £	Cropping £	Livestock £
Gross output per acre	102·4	77·2	50·3
Net farm income per acre	24·6	18·8	12·8
Farmer's and wife's labour per acre	12·8	10·1	10·8
Management and investment income per acre	11·8	8·7	2·0
Efficiency ratio	111·7	108·8	102·3

At a higher acreage level, the farmer's and wife's labour was relatively of much less importance.

Size-group 250—300 acres	Dairy £	Cropping £	Livestock £
Gross output per acre	81·9	61·2	38·7
Net farm income per acre	17·0	11·5	10·7
Farmer's and wife's labour per acre	2·6	2·0	2·7
Management and investment income per acre	14·4	9·5	8·0
Efficiency ratio	120·6	120·4	125·7

The Zuckerman report gave a graph showing the efficiency ratio calculated on a five-year average for the years 1952–56 for farms in the Farm Management Survey by size and type. This is reproduced in Figure 5.2.

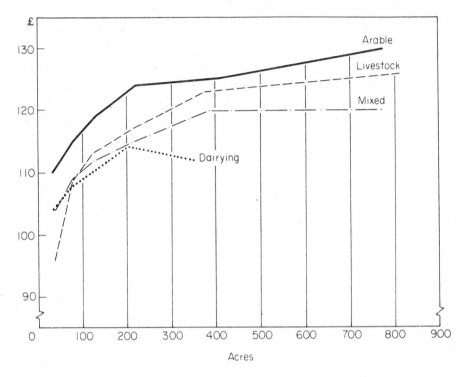

Fig. 5.2   Average gross output per £100 input (including labour of farmer and wife) by size and type of farm, England and Wales, 1952–56 (FMS sample)

Source: *Scale of Enterprise in Farming,* HMSO, 1961.

The resemblance to the 1970/71 situation depicted in Figure 5.1 is striking, and it is evident that little change occurred in the intervening fifteen years, either in the relationship between size and efficiency or in the differences between types of farming. The Zuckerman graph is somewhat more crudely drawn, as it appears to be based on only five or six broad size-groups compared with the thirteen groups used in preparing Figure 5.1, and it is likely that a closer analysis would have modified the conclusion that 'all types of farm (except dairy farms above 200 acres) show a *steady*[1] increase in the value of output per £100 of input as acreage increases'; but the 1970/71 results certainly reiterate the second Zuckerman conclusion that 'the rate of increase is greater in the smaller than in the larger size ranges for all types of farm, and it is also in the size-groups below 100 acres that the difference in the ratio between types of farms is greatest'.

Both studies indicate that efficiency tends to level off at a lower acreage for dairy farms than for cropping or livestock farms. But, above all, both confirm that, in general, the level of economic efficiency reached on farms of less than 200—250 acres (80—100 hectares) is very noticeably lower than on larger farms. The group of farms of 100—200 acres might be regarded as being, broadly speaking, in an intermediate stage between the struggling situation of the under-100 acre farms, most of which — in the terms of the Zuckerman report — are 'below the economic level of operation', and the more secure position of the majority of farms over 200 acres.

Statistical significance of differences in efficiency between size-groups

Because of the variation of individual farms around the average efficiency ratios shown in Table 5.1, it is of interest to apply a statistical test of significance to the differences between the efficiency ratios shown for the various groups.[2] It was found that, in the case of the 'all types' column of Table 5.1:

1 The average efficiency ratio was significantly lower for farms of 20—50 acres (99·9) than for farms in any of the higher size-groups.
2 The average efficiency ratio was also significantly lower for farms of 50—100 acres (108·9) than for farms in any of the higher size-groups.
3 The average efficiency ratio for farms of 100—150 acres was *not* significantly lower than for farms in all of the higher size-groups, though it was significantly lower than in some of those groups.
4 No significant difference occurred between the 100—150 and the 150—200 acre groups.
5 The average efficiency ratio for farms of 200—250 acres (120·3) was *not* significantly lower than for farms in any of the groups of over 250 acres, but it was significantly higher than for farms in any of the groups below it.

Thus these tests confirm the visual impression given by Figure 5.1 that, in England and Wales in 1970/71, farming efficiency, as measured by the efficiency ratio, did tend to increase significantly up to about 200—250 acres, but that for larger farms there was, on average, no significant improvement in efficiency.

For the farms of over 800 acres, larger samples than were available in the FMS in that year would be needed to establish whether or not the apparent improvement up to 1,000—1,200 acres and the deterioration thereafter were significant or were attributable to the chance effects of the sample.

Differences between size-groups within types of farm

As regards the differences within the types of farm shown in the subsequent columns of Table 5.1, it is interesting to note that for dairy farms there was no significant improvement in average efficiency beyond the 100—150 acre level, but significant improvements between the successive groups up to that level. The efficiency of livestock farms increased up to 100—150 acres, after which there was no further significant improvement until the 250—300 acre group was reached. Thereafter, this significantly better performance, compared with farms of 100—150 acres, was maintained up to the 400—500 acre level (and up to 500—600 on an 'adjusted acre' basis, when rough grazings are included with crops and grass by converting them to their equivalent pasture area). Efficiency improved significantly in cropping farms up to the 200—250 acre level, but there was no consistent trend thereafter. For instance, farms of 250—300 acres (average efficiency ratio 120·4) were not, on average, significantly more efficient than farms of 150—200 acres (116·3), nor were farms of 700—800 acres (126·7) significantly more efficient than farms of 200—250 acres (123·3). For the relatively few mixed farms in the FMS sample, there were significant improvements up to the 150—200 acre level, but not thereafter.

Summing up, we may say that the acreage beyond which significant improvements in efficiency did not appear to occur was 100—150 acres for dairy farms, 150—200 acres for mixed farms, 200—250 acres for cropping farms and 250—300 acres for livestock (cattle and/or sheep rearing) farms.

Differences between types of farming within size-groups

Looking at the FMS sample without regard to size, but considering only the respective types, it might be inferred from the overall averages for each type (dairy 115·4, livestock 113·1, cropping 120·3 and mixed 115·7) that cropping farms are generally the most efficient. This impression, however, is caused by the differences in size-composition of the samples, and does not emerge with any conviction when the types are compared with each other within specific size-groups, as given in Table 5.1.

Even the differences which did remain for 1970/71[3] should be interpreted with caution, as the absolute level of the efficiency ratio for a particular type of farming is liable to be greatly affected by the price farmers receive for their principal products. To some extent, the prices of inputs may produce a similar effect. Although these considerations may invalidate inter-type comparisons, they should not prevent fair comparison being made between farms of different sizes within types, or for all types taken together, which is our main concern.

Size and output per acre

Turning to some of the component items which affect the calculation of the efficiency ratio, the results for 1970/71 for all farms and for the different types of farms are summarised in Tables 5.2–5.6 and Figures 5.3–5.7.

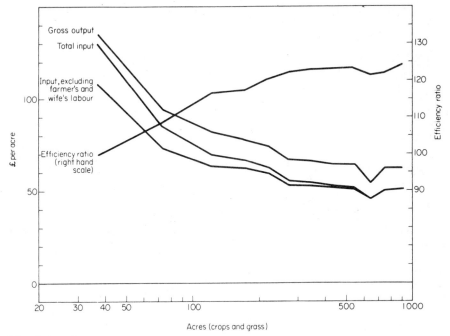

Fig. 5.3 Output and input per acre, and efficiency ratio, by size of farm, England and Wales, 1970/71, all farms (FMS)

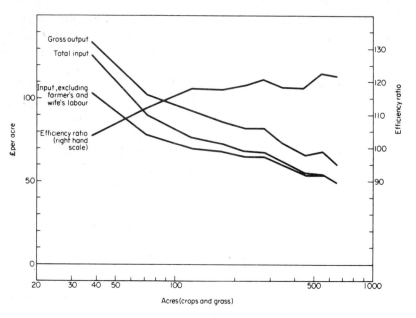

Fig. 5.4   Output and input per acre, and efficiency ratio, by size of farm, England and Wales, 1970/71, dairy farms (FMS)

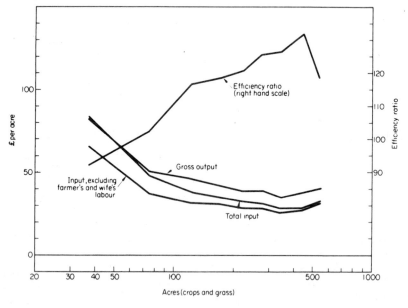

Fig. 5.5   Output and input per acre, and efficiency ratio, by size of farm, England and Wales, 1970/71, livestock farms (FMS)

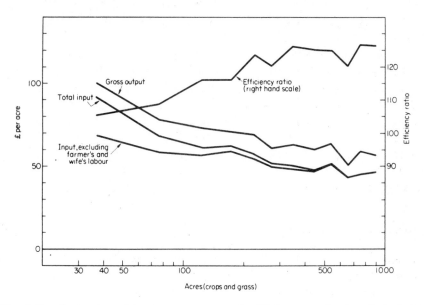

Fig. 5.6   Output and input per acre, and efficiency ratio, by size of farm,
England and Wales, 1970/71, cropping farms (FMS)

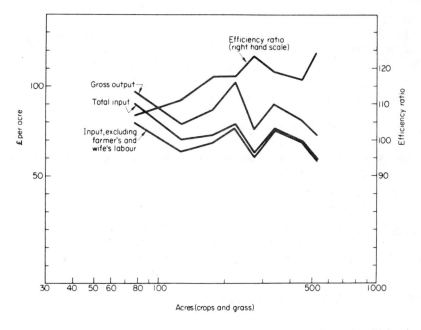

Fig. 5.7   Output and input per acre, and efficiency ratio, by size of farm,
England and Wales, 1970/71, mixed farms (FMS)

73

The Zuckerman Committee found that, on each type of farm, the value of gross output per acre fell as farm size increased (see Figure 5.2). This remained true in 1970/71, especially on dairy farms. This, as the Zuckerman report had noted, may be explained by the fact that small dairy farms make great use of purchased feedstuffs; the pattern of their *net* output in relation to size of farm is much like that for cropping farms.

In general, neither gross output nor net output per acre decline greatly on farms of over 300 acres, and, in the case of livestock farms, this figure would be nearer 200 acres. It would appear that large livestock-rearing farms do not have lower stocking densities per acre than medium-sized farms of the same type.

Size and inputs per acre

As regards total inputs, the Zuckerman Committee found, with the qualifications listed below (which apply also to the 1970/71 figures), that these combined inputs per acre fell steadily the larger the farm.[4] This was also generally true in 1970/71. Comparison between Tables 5.2—5.6 again shows that inputs are at a much lower level per acre on livestock farms than on other types. Another feature which is, if anything, even more pronounced in 1970/71 than in the earlier period, is that the decline in inputs per acre (other than the farmer's own labour) with size of farm is relatively insignificant on cropping farms. This may suggest that the larger cropping farms spend almost as much per acre on fertilisers, hired labour and machinery as do farms of about 100 acres.

The qualifications referred to above were:

(1) that nothing is charged for the management services of the farmer;
(2) that the manual labour of the farmer and his wife was charged in terms of their equivalent earnings over the same number of hours as agricultural workers. (See Appendix 2 to this chapter.) On small farms, the farmer's own labour is an important element in total input, and, as the Zuckerman Committee observed, any comparison between small and large farms which omitted this factor would be highly distorted;
(3) that no interest is charged on tenant's capital to compensate the farmer for his investment and for the risk attached to it.

Size, net farm income and management and investment income

Net farm income is probably the simplest measure of profitability in farming. It constitutes the surplus of total revenue over total expenditure,

74

Table 5.2

Output, income and tenant's capital per acre by size of farm,
England and Wales, 1970/71, all farms (FMS)[1]

Size-group (acres, crops and grass)	Number of farms	Average number of acres	Gross output	Net output[2]	Net farm income[3]	Farmer's and wife's labour	Management and investment income	Closing valuation[4]
					£ per acre			
20–	178	37	136	71	27·9	21·6	6·3	75
50–	494	74	94	59	21·2	11·7	9·5	60
100–	416	123	82	57	19·0	6·6	12·4	52
150–	319	173	78	55	15·8	4·6	11·2	52
200–	238	223	74	54	14·7	3·2	11·5	48
250–	184	274	67	53	14·1	2·4	11·7	46
300–	225	345	66	52	13·2	1·8	11·4	42
400–	148	443	64	50	12·7	1·2	11·5	40
500–	96	540	64	50	13·2	0·9	12·3	40
600–[5]	55	647	54	45	9·0	0·6	8·4	36
700–	29	747	62	53	12·6	0·4	12·2	38
800–	44	900	63	51	11·4	0·3	11·1	38
1,000–	12	1,057	58	50	12·2	0·2	12·0	33
1,200–	6	(1,294)	(63)	(52)	(10·5)	(0·2)	(10·3)	(35)
1,500 and over	12	1,844	52	44	8·2	0·1	8·1	40

[1] Excluding horticultural specialist holdings and part-time farms.

[2] Gross output less expenditure on feeds and seeds, adjusted for changes in stocks of these items.

[3] Net output less labour (except that of farmer and wife), rent and rates, machinery and power, fertilisers and other inputs.

[4] Breeding livestock valued at estimated market value; machinery, equipment, vehicles and tenant's fixtures valued at depreciated cost; trading livestock and crops valued at market value (fodder crops valued at cost); other physical stocks of short-term assets, and cultivations and residual manures. Land and buildings are not included.

[5] In the light of data for the other size-groups the figures for the 600–700 acre group appear to be somewhat anomalous. It seems that this group in the FMS sample contained a high proportion of farms producing mainly cereals, with a cropping intensity of only 4 smd per acre.

adjusted for the difference between opening and closing valuations of live-stock and crops. Because expenditure does not include any charge for the farmer's and wife's labour or managerial ability, the net farm income represents the material reward for their effort and capital invested.

75

Table 5.3
Output, income and tenant's capital per acre by size of farm, England and Wales, 1970/71, dairy farms (FMS)

Size-group (acres, crops and grass)	Number of farms	Average number of acres	Gross output	Net output[2]	Net farm income[3]	Farmer's and wife's labour	Management and investment income	Closing valuation[4]
					£ per acre			
20–	87	38	134	76	30·6	22·8	7·8	78
50–	262	72	102	65	24·6	12·7	11·9	66
100–	198	123	92	63	22·4	7·1	15·3	62
150–	136	172	86	59	18·2	4·9	13·3	59
200–	94	222	82	58	17·0	3·3	13·7	56
250–	56	276	82	61	17·0	2·6	14·4	57
300–	61	343	73	53	12·8	1·9	10·9	50
400–	32	448	66	52	11·9	1·1	10·8	49
500–	17	548	68	53	14·2	0·9	13·3	48
600–699	11	647	60	48	11·2	0·8	10·4	48

Footnotes: See previous Table.

Table 5.4
Output, income and tenant's capital per acre by size of farm, England and Wales, 1970/71, livestock farms (FMS)

Size-group (acres, crops and grass)	Number of farms	Average number of acres	Gross output	Net output[2]	Net farm income[3]	Farmer's and wife's labour	Management and investment income	Closing valuation[4]
					£ per acre			
20–	51	37	82	45	16·3	18·2	−1·9	69
50–	117	75	50	37	12·8	10·8	2·0	54
100–	98	121	46	36	14·2	6·7	7·5	49
150–	67	170	42	33	11·4	4·8	6·6	45
200–	48	220	39	32	10·3	3·6	6·7	45
250–	36	277	39	33	10·6	2·7	7·9	44
300–	31	343	35	30	9·1	2·3	6·8	38
400–	20	439	38	33	11·0	1·4	9·6	37
500–599	13	542	40	35	8·4	1·1	7·3	43

Footnotes: See Table 5.2.

Table 5.5
Output, income and tenant's capital per acre by size of farm, England and Wales, 1970/71, cropping farms (FMS)[1]

Size-group (acres, crops and grass)	Number of farms	Average number of acres	Gross output	Net output[2]	Net farm income[3]	Farmer's and wife's labour	Management and investment income	Closing valuation[4]
					£ per acre			
20–	21	37	100	80	31·7	23·5	8·2	32
50–	62	76	77	62	18·8	10·1	8·7	33
100–	78	125	73	60	16·7	5·5	11·2	33
150–	69	174	71	59	12·2	3·7	8·5	37
200–	76	225	69	57	14·5	2·7	11·8	36
250–	66	273	61	53	11·5	2·0	9·5	33
300–	97	348	63	55	14·4	1·8	12·6	32
400–	70	439	60	50	13·2	1·1	12·1	31
500–	52	540	64	52	13·6	0·8	12·8	34
600–[5]	35	648	51	44	8·2	0·5	7·7	31
700–	18	752	59	53	14·3	0·4	13·9	32
800–899	27	898	57	49	11·0	0·2	10·8	32

Footnotes: See Table 5.2.

Table 5.6
Output, income and tenant's capital per acre by size of farm, England and Wales, 1970/71, mixed farms (FMS)

Size-group (acres, crops and grass)	Number of farms	Average number of acres	Gross output	Net output[2]	Net farm income[3]	Farmer's and wife's labour	Management and investment income	Closing valuation[4]
					£ per acre			
50–	23	77	97	56	17·4	10·5	6·9	56
100–	29	126	79	52	15·2	6·7	8·5	47
150–	28	177	87	59	18·8	4·3	14·5	52
200–	14	224	102	62	15·8	2·8	13·0	58
250–	19	271	76	55	15·6	2·3	13·3	50
300–	30	339	90	62	14·9	1·5	13·4	57
400–	24	452	81	57	12·3	1·1	11·2	55
500–599	11	524	73	53	14·6	1·1	13·5	52

Footnotes: See Table 5.2.

The change in net farm income per acre with the increase in farm-size is shown in Figure 5.8 representing all farms in the 1970/71 sample. It shows an uninterrupted decline. As the graph and earlier tables show, on the smaller farms much of this net farm income is absorbed by the imputed charge for the farmer's and wife's own labour, and the remaining management and investment income per acre is very low. In 1970/71, it rose to an average of about £11 an acre when the 100-acre level was reached, and this figure showed little variation in the larger size-groups. Among dairy farms, management and investment income per acre appeared to reach its peak on farms of 100–150 acres.

Corresponding figures on a per farm (not per acre) basis are shown in Figures 5.9–5.12. The regular rise in total output corresponding with increasing acreage is clearly seen, as is the fairly steady accompanying rise

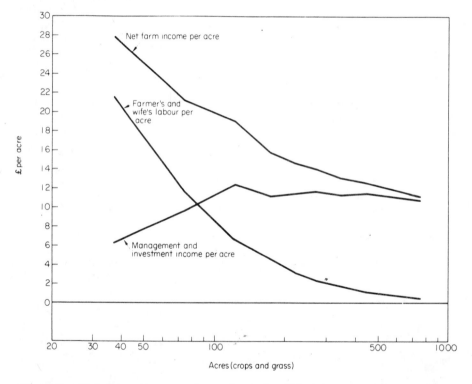

Fig. 5.8   Net farm income, farmer's and wife's labour and management and investment income per acre, by size of farm, England and Wales, 1970/71, all farms (excluding horticulture) (FMS)

Note: All farms of 500 acres and over have been treated as one group.

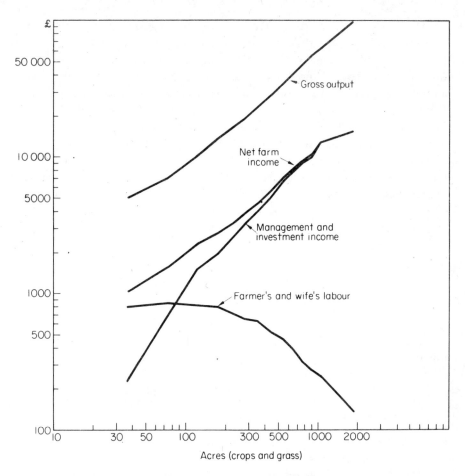

Fig. 5.9 Gross output, net farm income, management and investment income and farmer's and wife's labour by size of farm, England and Wales, 1970/71, all farms (excluding horticulture) (FMS)

in net farm income. Of much more interest, however, is the fact that, in 1970/71, farms of less than 100 acres generally earned a net farm income of less than £2,000, and at 50 acres the average was only a little over £1,200. On livestock farms (Figure 5.12), the corresponding figures were still lower — about £1,400 at 100 acres and £740 at 50 acres. Another notable feature of the livestock farm is that the estimated value of the farmer's and wife's labour is almost as high on a 500-acre farm as on a 50-acre farm; this is certainly not the case on other types of farm.

79

Once again, the 1970/71 figures appear to confirm the Zuckerman Committee's findings that, if net farm income is taken to represent the farmer's earnings, then the typical small farmer was earning less than a farm worker's wage. The Committee concluded that non-material rewards and sociological factors must have exerted a considerable influence on these farmers' determination not to give up, and although the analysis in Chapter 3 indicated that these farms are now tending to diminish in numbers year by year, it is clear that these influences are still powerful.

However, in this connection the fact that a farm family's total income from all sources is often considerably in excess of the calculated net farm income must not be overlooked. The expense of family labour, excepting

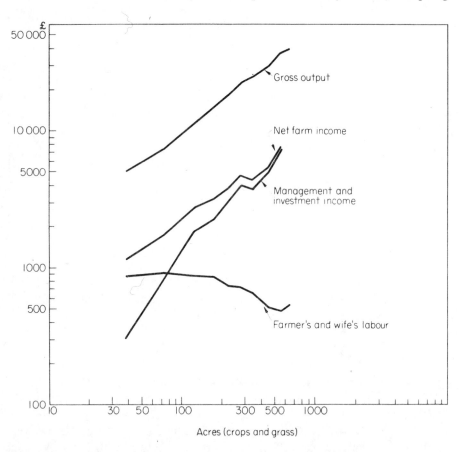

Fig. 5.10 Gross output, net farm income, management and investment income and farmer's and wife's labour by size of farm, England and Wales, 1970/71, dairy farms (FMS)

80

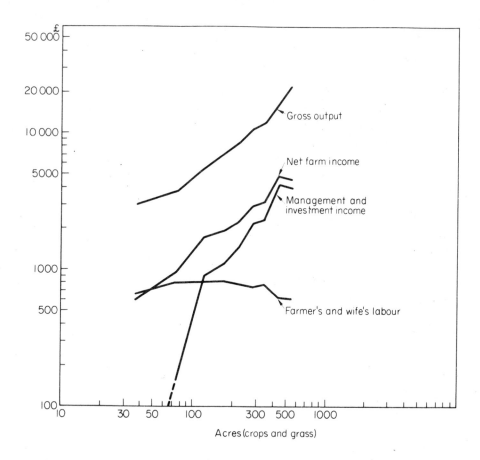

Fig. 5.11 Gross output, net farm income, management and investment income and farmer's and wife's labour by size of farm, England and Wales, 1970/71, livestock farms (FMS)

that of the farmer and his wife, is charged at current wage rates, but this charge becomes a part of total family income. One or more members of the family may also have considerable off-farm earnings. Another factor affecting the total financial position of owner-occupiers is that the market value of their land and other fixed assets may be increasing substantially year by year. This was certainly the case on many British farms until very recently.

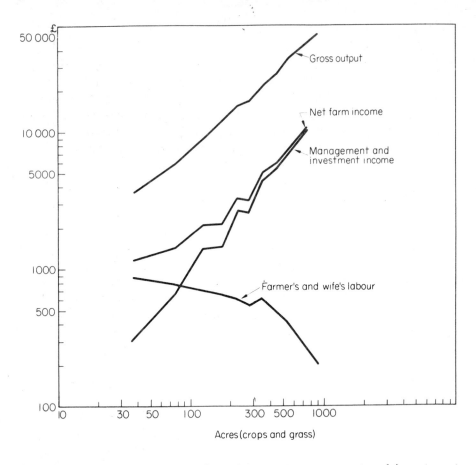

Fig. 5.12 Gross output, net farm income, management and investment income and farmer's and wife's labour by size of farm, England and Wales, 1970/71, cropping farms (FMS)

Variation of income within size-groups

We have no analysis available with respect to acreage size-groups that enables us to compare the income variability between farms in the various size-groups, but we have no reason to doubt the continuing validity of the Zuckerman Committee's observation that the relative spread of incomes tends to increase with size of farm. Their explanation that this is due to the fact that the earning possibilities of small farms are usually fairly narrowly prescribed, whereas there is a greater chance of earning a high income from a large farm where the opportunities are more diverse, still carries conviction.

82

Conclusion

On the basis of analysis by acreage size-groups, it is clear that *many farms of under 150 acres still suffer severe economic pressures which occur much less frequently in larger farms. The smaller farms often do not attain anything like a comparable level of output in relation to the resources used, and when this is combined with the limitations imposed by size itself, their monetary rewards are frequently very low.* This is probably the major factor leading to the structural changes which have already taken place, and further change in the same direction — that is, towards the enlargement of farm areas — can be expected.

Size of business (in smd) and efficiency

A broad indication of the relationship between size of business and efficiency has already been given in Table 3.6, when we were considering what proportion of the national output, input, net income and tenant's capital is to be found in different sizes of farm business. The table clearly showed that the group of holdings of 275 to 599 smd's — that is, the smallest holdings qualifying for the description 'full-time farm business' — account for nearly 18 per cent of agricultural output and use about 20 per cent of the land and capital, and that, on average, they operate at an appreciably lower level of efficiency than the larger holdings.

Further indications of the relationship are given each year in *Farm Incomes in England and Wales.* For example, the following figures, taken from the 1972/73 edition of that publication, indicate that among a group of the same 2,000 farms for two successive years, average efficiency (as measured by output per £100 input) was lowest in the group of smallest farm businesses, rose to a maximum in the middle range of 1,200–2,399 smd's, and then declined slightly among the larger businesses of the 2,400–4,199 smd group.

Size of business (smd)	Number of farms	Gross output per £100 input (including value of farmer's and wife's labour)	
		1971/72	1972/73
275–599	409	121	129
600–1,199	750	129	137
1,200–1,799	419	130	139
1,800–2,399	217	130	139
2,400–4,199	205	127	133
Average	2,000	127	136

The relationship has not been so consistent in all recent years, but the same general pattern has tended to recur not only between years but also in the various types of farming which the MAFF distinguishes in the FMS sample.

Making use of the tape which was available to us containing the data for 1970/71 (see p.4.) we analysed the size/efficiency relationship in more detail. The results of this analysis are summarised in Table 5.7.

The table confirms the rapid climb in average efficiency as business size increases from 300–600 smd, with a slower increase thereafter, a suggestion of a peak at 1,200–1,500 smd and some evidence of a decline in the largest farms of over 4,200 smd. This is shown graphically in Figure 5.13.

From the data given in Table 5.7, certain points can be observed. It is clear that the larger businesses generate considerably more output per acre (in terms of monetary value) than the smaller businesses, but without using proportionately more inputs. If farms of 400–600 smd and farms of 1,500–2,400 smd are compared, it will be seen that although the larger farms obtained about £11 more output per acre than the smaller, the

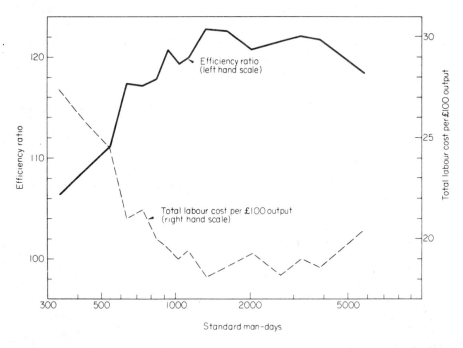

Fig. 5.13   Average efficiency ratio on farms of different sizes of business, England and Wales, 1970/71

Table 5.7
Size of business and efficiency, England and Wales, 1970/71

Size of business (smd)	Number of farms	Efficiency ratio	Acres (crops and grass)	Intensity		Total labour cost (£)			Tenant's capital £ per acre
				£ output per acre	£ input per acre	per acre	per smd	per £100 output	
300—	143	106·4	76	55	52	15·1	3·36	27·4	37
400—	154	109·0	84	59	54	15·0	2·87	25·6	43
500—	170	111·2	105	60	54	14·7	2·85	24·5	44
600—	192	117·4	122	63	55	13·2	2·54	21·0	42
700—	179	117·2	147	62	53	13·3	2·64	21·4	42
800—	132	117·8	155	67	56	13·3	2·47	20·0	46
900—	122	120·7	177	67	56	13·1	2·46	19·6	43
1,000—	136	119·4	219	60	49	11·3	2·38	19·0	41
1,100—	132	120·0	207	67	57	13·0	2·37	19·4	44
1,200—	237	122·8	252	68	56	12·4	2·35	18·1	42
1,500—	189	122·6	294	70	57	13·1	2·36	18·6	44
1,800—	240	120·8	370	71	59	13·7	2·46	19·3	43
2,400—	129	121·6	469	75	61	13·6	2·39	18·2	43
3,000—	59	122·1	541	79	66	15·1	2·51	19·0	45
3,600—	34	121·7	673	80	67	15·0	2·60	18·6	43
4,200 and over	82	118·4	847	82	70	16·8	2·43	20·5	45

difference in input was only about £4 per acre. The amount of tenant's capital per acre was practically the same in these groups.

Looking at the figures for labour cost (including the farmer's and wife's labour), it is evident that the farms in the smaller size-groups use appreciably more labour per acre than the medium-sized farms, yet they achieve less output. The combined effect is that labour cost per £100 output is much higher on the farms of under 600 smd than on the farms above this size. The most efficient size in this respect seems to lie between 1,200 and 3,000 smd (see Figure 5.13). The figures strongly suggest that there is a high degree of correlation between labour productivity and the efficient use of total inputs.

The suggestion of a possible diseconomy of size beyond about 4,000 smd, corresponding to a farm employing about 15 men, should also be noted. However, a more comprehensive study of farms at that end of the scale than is possible from the FMS sample would be needed before any firm conclusions could be drawn.

The average efficiency ratios in each size-group for each of the main types of farming are shown in Table 5.8. On the whole, the figures reveal the same kind of size/efficiency relationship in each type group.

Table 5.8
Average efficiency ratios by size of business and
type of farming

Size of business (smd)	Dairy farms	Livestock farms	Cropping farms
300–	106·7	105·0	109·5
400–	110·9	105·8	111·5
500–	109·8	113·6	111·2
600–	116·3	117·6	121·1
700–	113·3	120·8	122·2
800–	116·2	122·3	119·5
900–	119·6	123·5	124·9
1,000–	116·0	122·0	126·4
1,100–	117·3	126·5	122·6
1,200–	120·3	132·2	126·6
1,500–	121·3	125·8	124·1
1,800–	119·8	123·3	120·9
2,400–	118·8	n.a.	125·1
3,000–	120·9	n.a.	127·0
3,600–	n.a.	n.a.	121·6
4,200 and over	120·8	n.a.	120·1

Variation in efficiency between farm businesses of the same size

In all the foregoing analysis, a great deal of use has been made of *average* performance in each size-group, and comments have been made about the evidence of some systematic relationships between these averages. It must, however, be emphasised that farms within each size-group vary greatly in efficiency. Those who work in the advisory services make frequent reference to the wide gap which exists between the average and the best in British agriculture, and the FMS data show that this is true at all levels of size of business and in all types of farming.

Looking first at the 1970/71 records available for the whole sample of farms in England and Wales, we find the frequency distribution of efficiency ratios as shown in the last line of Table 5.9.

Table 5.9
Percentage distribution of efficiency ratios in each smd group,
England and Wales, 1970/71

Size of business (smd)	Less than 50	50–	60–	70–	80–	90–	100–	110–	120–	130–	140–	150–	160 and over
Less than 300	1·6	6·1	9·5	14·0	16·8	17·9	11·7	14·0	4·5	2·8	0·6	0·6	–
300–399	–	–	0·8	5·4	10·1	21·7	21·7	22·5	10·1	3·9	2·3	–	1·6
400–499	0·6	1·2	–	1·8	5·3	17·8	28·4	22·5	13·0	5·3	3·0	0·6	0·6
500–599	–	–	0·6	3·7	6·7	11·0	23·2	28·1	14·0	7·3	3·7	1·8	–
600–699	–	–	0·5	0·5	3·0	11·1	20·6	27·1	17·1	9·0	5·0	2·5	3·5
700–799	–	–	0·6	0·6	2·3	12·1	19·7	23·1	20·8	12·1	5·2	0·6	2·9
800–899	–	–	–	0·7	4·4	3·0	23·0	21·5	31·9	9·6	5·2	0·7	–
900–999	–	–	–	–	4·1	8·3	14·9	23·1	19·8	15·7	8·3	3·3	2·5
1,000–1,099	–	–	–	0·8	1·5	6·8	27·3	20·5	17·4	11·4	8·3	3·0	3·0
1,100–1,199	–	–	–	–	1·5	8·4	20·6	26·7	18·3	9·9	7·6	2·3	4·6
1,200–1,499	–	–	–	0·4	1·7	6·1	16·0	22·9	22·1	15·2	7·4	4·8	3·5
1,500–1,799	–	–	–	–	0·5	4·8	14·9	24·5	26·6	17·0	7·4	2·1	2·1
1,800–2,399	–	–	–	0·4	0·8	6·7	17·5	27·5	20·8	15·0	7·9	2·1	1·3
2,400–2,999	–	–	–	–	0·8	2·4	16·9	24·2	34·7	12·9	4·8	2·4	0·8
3,000–3,599	–	–	–	–	–	5·1	18·6	20·3	30·5	11·9	10·2	3·4	–
3,600–4,199	–	–	–	–	–	5·9	17·6	20·6	26·5	23·5	5·9	–	–
4,200 and over	–	–	–	–	–	8·5	20·7	29·3	23·2	8·5	6·1	2·4	1·2
Total (weighted average)[1]	0·1	0·5	0·9	1·8	3·4	9·4	19·3	24·1	20·5	10·7	5·7	2·0	1·6

[1] The percentages were calculated from data for each separate smd group, these then being weighted according to their relative importance in the total smd in England and Wales (census data). The figures may therefore be regarded as estimates of the distribution for the country as a whole, after correcting for the somewhat distorted size-distribution of the FMS sample.

This distribution is reproduced on the 'All farms' section of Figure 5.14, from which it will be seen that it approximates to the normal distribution of statistical theory, being roughly symmetrical around the mean of 118 and having progressively smaller frequencies the greater the distance from the mean.

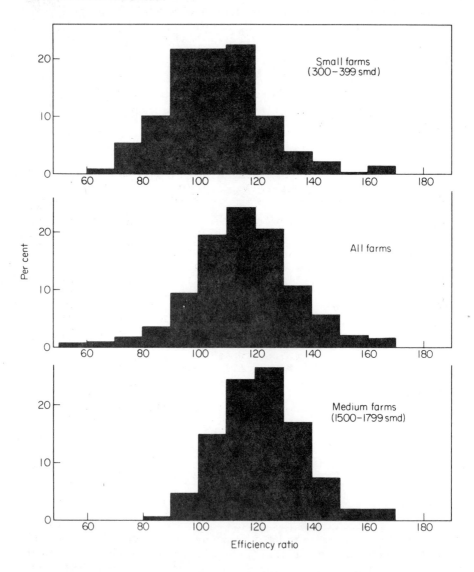

Fig. 5.14   Frequency distribution of farms according to efficiency ratios, England and Wales, 1970/71

The fact that the small farms tend, on average, to be less efficient than the medium-sized farms is also shown in Figure 5.14 where, despite their wide spread, the small farms tend to cluster around a value of 100–110 while the medium-sized farms have their peak frequency at about 125.

An analysis taking account of the degree of variation in efficiency within 16 successive size-groups is shown in Figure 5.15, which gives the median value of the efficiency ratio for the farms in each group, together with the values of the first and third quartiles (below and above which, respectively, fell 25 per cent of the recorded farms in 1970/71). It is interesting to see that the extent of variation between farms seems to be about the same at all levels of size of business. The inter-quartile range is generally just under 20 per cent of the median value, irrespective of size. In other words, about half of the farms fall outside the range of 10 per cent either side of the median level of efficiency.

If we describe farms with an output/input ratio of less than 100 as 'low-efficiency' farms and those with a ratio of 130 or more as

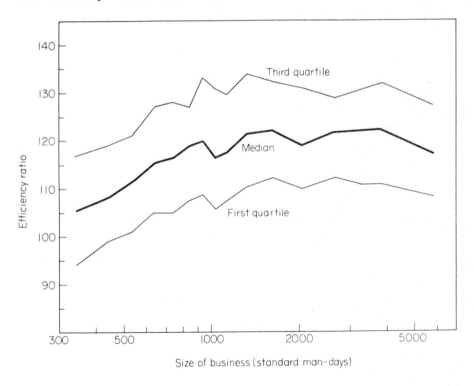

Fig. 5.15   Range of efficiency ratios associated with different levels of size of business, England and Wales, 1970/71

'high-efficiency' farms, it is possible to study the changing proportions of these two categories at different levels of business size. This is shown in Figure 5.16, where the curves have been drawn freehand through the points obtained from the data. Among the smallest farms (under 500 smd), the low-efficiency farms greatly outnumber the high-efficiency farms, but the proportions change rapidly with increasing size, and at 700 smd they are equal, with 17 per cent in each category. Thereafter the proportion of high-efficiency farms rises until a size of about 1,400 smd (the five-man farm) is reached, after which it declines. The proportion of low-efficiency farms appears to decline throughout the size-range as size increases.

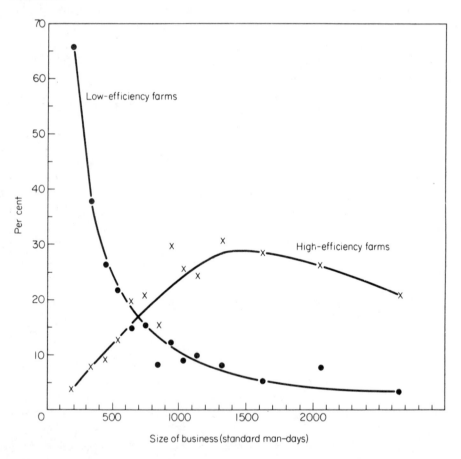

Fig. 5.16 Percentage of low-efficiency and high-efficiency farms at different levels of size of business, England and Wales, 1970/71

Somewhat more recent data on the disparities in efficiency between farms of different sizes and types may be extracted from the report on *Farm Incomes in England and Wales 1972–73*. Table 5.10 relates the efficiency ratios of MAFF's 'high performance' farms to those of 'low performance' farms in each group. The definitions of these categories are as follows. Farms were ranked according to their output per £100 input, including the farmer's and wife's labour, averaged over the two years 1971/72 and 1972/73. The quarter of the farms with the highest ratios were classed as 'high performance' and the quarter with the lowest as 'low performance'. The table indicates that, in most groups, the top quarter of farms were at least 40 per cent more efficient than the bottom quarter, on the basis of this measurement of efficiency. The gap seems to have been widest among the livestock-rearing farms (cattle and sheep).

Table 5.10

Ratio of average of top 25 per cent ('high performance') to average of bottom 25 per cent ('low performance') farms in level of efficiency, England and Wales, 1972/73

Size of business (smd)	Dairy farms	Livestock farms	Cropping farms	Mixed farms
275–599	1·53	1·60	1·49	1·54
600–1,199	1·44	1·82	1·46	1·33
1,200–1,799	1·41	1·80	1·45	1·33
1,800–2,399	1·45	1·66	1·42	n.a.
2,400–4,199	1·37	n.a.	1·45	1·33
Average	1·44	1·72	1·45	1·35

Source: *Farm Incomes in England and Wales 1972–73*, Tables 61–4.

The turning-point for economies of size

A number of the tables and diagrams reproduced in this chapter indicate that the diseconomies of small size appear to operate rather severely below about 600 smd, while above about 1,000 smd there is no very strong evidence of any further economies being gained. It is also noticeable that, above the size of 600 smd, the farmer and his wife tend to do progressively less farm work.

These observations suggest that there is a kind of intermediate or transitional size of 600–1,000 smd at which the handicaps experienced by small farms become somewhat easier to overcome. It seems that, in 1970/71, the three-man farm (about 800–850 smd) stood a good chance of being just as efficient, in terms of output per unit of input, as the larger farms.

It is perhaps more than a coincidence that this apparent turning-point in economies of size at about 800–850 smd corresponds to the size of business at which total wages earned by paid labour begins to exceed the estimated value of unpaid labour. Figure 5.17 shows that the proportion which paid labour bears to the total labour cost rises steadily with size of business and reaches 50 per cent at about 800 smd (that is, the three-man farm).

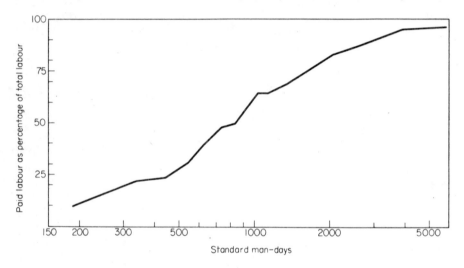

Fig. 5.17 Cost of paid labour as percentage of total labour by size of business, England and Wales, 1970/71

It might be supposed that this 50 per cent point marks the distinction between 'family farms' and other farms, since thereafter paid labour tends to predominate. However, the situation is complicated by the fact that the FMS includes members of the family under 'paid labour', if they receive a regular wage. 'Unpaid labour' is therefore generally less than the total family contribution to the labour force.

Size of business and profitability

In Chapter 2 it was pointed out that although from the point of view of the optimum use of national resources the important economies of size are those which lead to a higher output/input ratio, from the point of view of the individual farmer this ratio will be of less consequence than his net profit. It is therefore of interest to analyse economies of size in terms of the average profitability associated with different sizes of business. Table 5.11 gives the results of such an analysis for 1970/71. Profitability is measured by calculating the management and investment income as a percentage of the tenant's capital valuation, and also by making the same calculation after allowing for the farmer's imputed salary payment, this allowance varying with the size of business.[5]

Table 5.11

Size of business and profitability —
average values (£'000) in each size-group, England and
Wales, 1970/71

Size of business (smd)	Gross output	Net farm income	Farmer's and wife's labour	Management and investment income	Tenant's capital	Imputed management salary	Return on capital (per cent)	
							Before deducting salary	After deducting salary
300–	4·23	1·05	0·79	0·26	2·77	0·31	9·4	−1·9
400–	4·93	1·25	0·85	0·40	3·60	0·37	11·1	0·9
500–	6·29	1·46	0·84	0·62	4·59	0·49	13·5	2·6
600–	7·71	1·87	0·82	1·05	5·13	0·59	20·5	8·9
700–	9·13	2·20	0·80	1·40	6·22	0·74	22·5	10·6
800–	10·35	2·55	0·84	1·71	7·19	0·84	23·8	12·2
900–	11·81	2·74	0·77	1·97	7·54	0·94	26·1	13·6
1,000–	13·01	2·94	0·71	2·23	9·05	1·06	24·6	12·9
1,100–	13·92	2·99	0·78	2·21	9·13	1·14	24·2	11·7
1,200–	17·19	3·82	0·72	3·10	10·60	1·40	29·2	16·0
1,500–	20·68	4·47	0·67	3·80	12·94	1·75	29·4	15·8
1,800–	26·26	4·89	0·63	4·26	16·08	2·19	26·5	12·9
2,400–	35·03	6·75	0·53	6·22	20·26	2·93	30·7	16·3
3,000–	43·00	7·96	0·48	7·48	24·38	3·67	30·7	15·6
3,600–	54·16	9·34	0·31	9·03	28·76	4·38	31·4	16·1
4,200 and over	69·42	10·67	0·25	10·42	38·04	5·85	27·4	12·1

The table shows that the average return on tenant's capital was much lower on farms of less than 600 smd than it was on larger farms. The diseconomies of size, as reflected in the rate of profitability, appear to have been largely eliminated when the size of business reached about 900 smd, but there was still some tendency for the rate of profit to increase with size thereafter and the highest average rates (exceeding 30 per cent return on capital, or 16 per cent if a salary allowance is deducted) occurred after the 1,200 smd level had been passed.

It is interesting to see how steadily the management and investment income increases with size of business, but the amount of tenant's capital also increases. A large business may thus have two or three times more net income than a smaller business, but will not necessarily have a higher rate of return on invested capital.

It may also be seen that the apparently low rates of return obtained on the farms of under 600 smd cannot be explained away by a suggestion that the allowance for the farmer's and wife's labour is unrealistically high. Even if the allowance were reduced to half the amount recorded, there would still be a substantially lower average rate of profitability on these smaller farms than is observed further up the size scale.

Table 5.12
Return on capital (after deducting an allowance
for management salary) and associated variables,
England and Wales 1970/71

Return on capital (per cent)	Per cent of farms	Average size of farm			Average valuation (tenant's capital), £'000	Total labour per £100 gross output	Farmer's and wife's labour per £100 total labour
		Smd	Crops and grass (acres)	Gross output, £'000			
−100 or more	1·0	303	67	3·7	0·90	32·2	55·1
−50 to −100	2·8	589	106	6·0	3·06	32·9	34·5
−30 to −50	3·5	961	139	10·5	5·07	25·9	24·5
−20 to −30	4·2	859	154	9·6	5·84	25·9	29·7
−10 to −20	7·8	1,055	192	11·8	7·76	25·3	23·1
−5 to −10	5·7	1,221	224	14·4	9·51	22·1	23·2
0 to −5	7·3	1,328	235	15·4	11·35	22·1	21·9
0 to 5	9·7	1,284	222	14·8	9·87	21·9	23·1
5−10	9·4	1,364	236	16·7	11·42	20·5	21·2
10−15	10·4	1,356	245	16·3	11·50	19·5	24·2
15−20	8·8	1,586	284	19·1	13·12	18·5	21·0
20−30	13·8	1,506	275	20·1	12·38	18·0	20·0
30−40	6·9	1,581	290	23·0	12·44	17·0	16·8
40−50	3·2	1,478	258	21·2	10·14	17·0	17·4
50−75	3·3	1,443	288	22·2	8·76	14·7	18·3
75−100	1·0	1,744	351	31·2	8·31	13·3	12·2
100−200	0·9	1,263	265	20·9	4·67	15·5	19·2
Over 200[1]	0·2	(917)	(198)	(12·8)	(1·57)	(13·6)	(36·1)

[1]   Only five farms in this group.

Variation between farms in rate of return on capital

An analysis has been made of the frequency of occurrence of different rates of return on tenant's capital (after deducting a salary allowance), and of the average values of other farm characteristics associated with the different rates. The results of this analysis for 1970/71 are shown in Table 5.12. The following points may be observed:

1 There was a very wide dispersion of rates of return, and these were fairly symmetrically distributed around the highest frequency at 10–15 per cent (allowing for the fact that the group from 20–30 per cent is twice as wide in its range).

2 Low profitability was highly correlated with low size of farm, whether size is measured in acres, smd or value of gross output. The highest rates of profitability tended to be associated with farms of over 250 acres and of over 1,400 smd.

3 The amount of tenant's capital showed no regular relationship with level of profitability. Farms with high profitability appeared to use their tenant's capital per acre and per £100 output less intensively than farms with average profitability.

4 Labour costs absorbed a higher proportion of the value of output on the low-profit farms than on the high-profit farms. This was a noticeably regular relationship.

5 Farmer's and wife's labour constituted a high proportion of the total labour cost on the least profitable farms.

95

Appendix 1: evidence from Sweden

Some results presented by Gulbrandsen and Lindbeck[6] confirm many of the conclusions drawn from the analysis of British data. They noted, of course, the strong correlation between farm acreage and farm income, at the same time pointing out that, on the smallest farms, a considerable additional sum is earned outside the farm itself, the farmer being employed part-time elsewhere. They went on to examine the relationship between profitability and acreage, defining profitability as the labour return per hour worked, after deducting an interest charge for the input of the farmer's own capital. They found that, in the range from 5 to 50 hectares, 'labour return . . . definitely rises in proportion to the acreage'.

Next, they considered the actual profitability of a farm with a certain labour input (say 5,000 hours per year) compared with what could have been achieved in the same year by 'the optimally adapted farm' using the techniques available at the time. In 1960, this 'optimal farm' would have covered about 120–150 hectares (instead of the existing 20–30 hectares) and would then have been capable of increasing its labour return per hour roughly fourfold. They also noted that a study by Hjelm had shown that there were 'practically no topographical impediments in Sweden to a transition to farms of 100 hectares or more' (p. 57). However, they were doubtful about the acceptability of the 'optimal' calculations because they presupposed that at least one member of each farm family would possess the 'extremely high managerial qualities' necessary to achieve the optimal results. For this reason, they considered that the figures indicating a fourfold increase in profitability 'exaggerate the ability of the family farm to improve its profitability by increasing its acreage' (p. 57). Hjelm has also remarked that 'an enlargement of farms by amalgamation of smaller farms will probably not give better profitability unless it is combined with an increasing capacity of the manager . . . Size rationalisation must be combined with rational management practices if the new technology is to be utilised in an economic way.'[7]

We would suggest that this objection is not as strong as it may appear at first sight for, if the existing farms of 20–30 hectares became amalgamated into farms of 120–150 hectares, presumably only one in five or six of the existing families would remain in farming and if the process of selection was such that the best farmers remained in the business, the necessary managerial ability might reasonably be expected to manifest itself.

Gulbrandsen and Lindbeck also give support to the concept of the shifting optimum, suggesting that, if the techniques envisaged by Hjelm became available by 1975, an optimally adapted farm in the southern Swedish plains would require 320 hectares.

Looking at the relative profitability of farms of different sizes, instead of calculating the ratio of output to input (O)/(I), they related 'profit' (O−I) to the capital value of the farm business, including the value of the land. As in the UK, they found that if the labour of the farmer and his family is included as an input, 'profit' is negative for many small farms. Using data for 1966, their analysis showed that, on average, this negative character-istic was rapidly reduced as size increased from 5 hectares to 20 hectares, at which point 'profit' was about zero. Thereafter, profitability in relation to capital value continued to increase with size of farm, but at a diminishing rate, eventually levelling off at about 50 hectares. The authors pointed out, however, that, by including land value in the total capital, the ratio which they calculated was difficult to interpret, because 'if profits rise . . . the market value of the farm rises too' (p. 69). When they substituted for the market value an alternative use value (forestry) which was not affected by agricultural profitability, they found there was no levelling-off with increasing size − at least not up to about 100 hectares, which was the limit of the range of the study.

Summing up on economies of scale in agriculture, they say that 'the small units of today include far too little land and livestock in relation to the supply of labour, plant and machinery. The existing structure, with its small acreages (mean acreage 19 hectares) and small herds (average 8 cows and 30 pigs), does not admit of anything like the optimum factor proportions in agriculture . . . A radical increase in the size of farms . . . could therefore be expected to pave the way to higher productivity'.[6]

Appendix 2: farmer's and wife's labour

Because so many of the agricultural holdings in England and Wales are worked by one or two men (one of whom is the farmer himself) with some occasional help from others (one of whom is likely to be the farmer's wife), any attempt to measure the efficiency of the use of resources on farms of different sizes must take due account of the item described in the farm accounts as 'farmer's and wife's labour'.

The importance of including this item in the analysis lies not so much in its absolute amount as in its relative predominance among the total inputs on small farms and its relative insignificance on large farms. The Zuckerman report clearly pointed out that to omit the farmer's own labour when comparing the efficiency of small and large farms would lead to 'heavily distorted' results. It stated (p. 19) that in 1955 the data by size-groups showed that, for all farms below 50 acres, the unpaid labour of the farmer and his wife accounted for more than half of the total manual labour input; and again (p. 30), it noted that although the total cost of all kinds of labour per unit of output is reasonably constant over the range of farm sizes, 'there is . . . a very large drop . . . in the contribution of the farmer's own labour per unit of output as size of farm increases'; and commented, 'this is probably the most significant feature brought out by the analysis.'

The persistence of this feature is brought out in Tables 5.13 and 5.14 as well as in Figure 5.18.

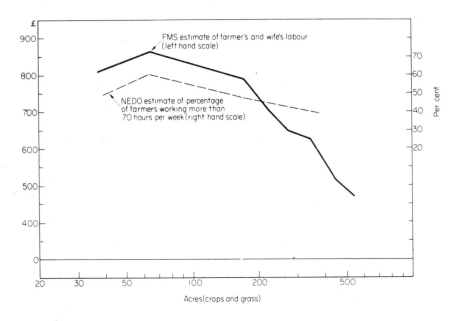

Fig. 5.18 Relationship between size of farm and amount of farmer's and wife's labour

The sources of information on the amount and value of the farmer's and wife's labour deserve some scrutiny, as it will be evident from the figures given above that the omission of this item is not only bound to lead to distorted comparisons, but any substantial overestimation or under-estimation could also impair the validity of conclusions about relative efficiency or relative levels of profitability (management and investment income, or rate of return on capital).

98

Table 5.13
Farmer's and wife's labour in relation to gross
output and net farm income by size of farm
(acres, crops and grass), England and Wales, 1970/71,
all farms (FMS)[1]

Size-group (acres, crops and grass)	Farmer's and wife's labour	
	Per £100 gross output	Per £100 net farm income
20–	15·9	77·5
50–	12·5	55·4
100–	8·1	35·0
150–	5·9	28·9
200–	4·3	21·5
250–	3·5	16·8
300–	2·7	13·7
400–	1·8	9·1
500–599	1·4	6·6

[1] Excluding horticultural specialist holdings and part-time farms.

Table 5.14
Farmer's and wife's labour in relation to gross output
and net farm income by size of business (smd),
England and Wales, 1970/71, all farms (FMS)[1]

Size-group (smd)	Farmer's and wife's labour		
	Per £100 gross output	Per £100 net farm income	Per £100 total labour
300	31·4	145·0	84·5
300–	18·9	75·3	69·4
400–	17·2	67·9	67·1
500–	13·4	57·9	54·7
600–	10·7	43·9	50·7
700–	8·8	36·4	41·1
800–	8·1	32·8	40·4
900–	6·5	28·0	33·2
1,000–	5·5	24·2	28·8
1,100–	5·6	26·2	29·1
1,200–	4·2	18·8	23·0
1,500–	3·2	15·0	17·5
1,800–	2·4	12·9	12·4
2,400–	1·5	7·8	8·3
3,000–	1·1	6·0	5·9
3,600–	0·6	3·3	3·1
4,200 and over	0·4	2·4	1·8

[1] Excluding horticultural specialist holdings and part-time farms.

In the Farm Management Survey, the item is estimated for accounting purposes 'by valuing the estimated time worked by the farmer and his wife at the appropriate paid labour rates'.[8] No estimate for managerial, secretarial or clerical activity is included in this figure. The average value per farm, in comparison with the annual earnings of hired men doing regular full-time work on the farm, has risen as follows:

Year	Farmer's and wife's labour £	Annual earnings of hired men £
1969/70	700	952
1970/71	782	1,062
1971/72	887	1,186
1972/73	978	1,386

This comparison would seem to suggest that farmers and their wives are working fewer hours than their hired men (if we may assume that the 'appropriate paid labour rates' being applied to the farmers are not less than the hourly rates they are paying their men). On the other hand, there is other evidence which suggests that this is far from being the case. A survey of 4,768 farmers in England and Wales carried out in 1970 by the National Economic Development Office (with the help of Agricultural Economics departments of universities) asked the question: 'How many hours do you spend in a week on work related to your holding on average over the year?' The average answer was 63·8 hours per week (3,318 hours per year). The farmers were also asked: 'Roughly over the year how much of your (working) time do you spend doing clerical, administrative or supervisory work?' The average answer to this question was 11·3 per cent of working time. This means that, according to this survey, farmers worked manually on their farms an average of 56·6 hours per week (2,943 hours per year[9]). This excludes any allowance for work done by their wives, which was recorded separately (see p.102). In the same survey, 4,834 regular farm workers were asked how many hours, including over-time, they worked per week on average over the year, and the average reply was 52·2 hours. (On the NEDO assumption of a 48-week year, this implies 2,506 hours per year.)

Thus the NEDO survey would suggest that farmers generally work a longer working week than their men, and that even when clerical, administrative and supervisory work are excluded, they still put in an average of 4·4 hours more manual work per week than the average of their

100

men. If this is indeed the case, then it would seem that the FMS under-states the value of this work, especially as the work of farmers' wives is also included in the FMS estimates. However, the NEDO does not place great reliance on the answers given. The report states that 'there may have been a tendency by the farmer to slightly overestimate his hours. Most farmers live where they work and this made it particularly difficult to determine the exact time spent working'.

Another source of information about the amount of work done by farmers is to be found in the report on *Availability of capital and credit to United Kingdom agriculture* prepared for the Ministry of Agriculture, Fisheries and Food by Professor J.S.G. Wilson (The Wilson Report). In 1971, a random sample of farmers (excluding very large and very small farms, and also excluding horticulture) were asked: 'What would you consider a suitable charge for your own manual labour?' From the 345 replies, the average figure was £1,134 per farmer per year. This is 45 per cent higher than the average of £782 given by the FMS for farmer's *and* wife's labour for 1970/71. The Wilson Report mentions, however, that some farmers declared a very high figure — in one instance £4,500, and this was supposed to exclude the value of 'managerial effort', which was separately returned — and that 'many of the estimates really only amount to a rough guess'. A round figure of £1,000 was given by 86 of the 345 replies.

On the whole, it seems reasonable to have more confidence in the much larger NEDO sample, all of whom were personally interviewed, than in the Wilson Report sample, some of whom were not interviewed but replied by post.

In certain respects the NEDO results confirm those of the FMS, notably in the variation between types of farming and between sizes of farm. Both surveys showed that dairy farmers and livestock farmers work, on average, more hours on their farms than do other farmers, while cropping farmers work fewer hours (Table 5.15). Figure 5.18 shows a close relationship between the NEDO analysis of the percentage of farmers working more than 70 hours per week in the various acreage size-groups, and the FMS analysis of the value of farmer's and wife's labour, also by farm acreage.

If we place some degree of confidence in the NEDO figures of average hours of manual labour worked by farmers (56·6 hours per week), and apply to them the average earnings reported for hired men in England and Wales in 1969/70 (37·7p per hour) we arrive at an estimate of £1,110 per year. This lends some credence to the Wilson Report average of £1,134. If we add some £130 for the work of the farmer's wife (see p.105), this gives

Table 5.15
Farmer's own labour on different types of farm,
England and Wales (NEDO survey 1970 and FMS 1970/71)

Type of farming	NEDO survey 1970		FMS 1970/71	
	Weekly hours worked by farmer	Index, total = 100	Farmer's and wife's labour (£ per year)	Index total = 100
Dairy	61·8	109	862[2]	110
Livestock	58·8	104	814[3]	104
Pigs/poultry	51·4	91	757	97
Cropping	48·6	86	621[4]	79
Mixed	56·6	100	719	92
Total	56·6[1]	100	782	100

[1] Including horticulture.
[2] Average of specialist dairy and mainly dairy.
[3] Average of livestock, mostly sheep and livestock, cattle and sheep.
[4] Average of cropping, mostly cereals and general cropping.

a total of £1,240 for 1969/70, compared with the FMS average of £700 for that year. If £1,240 is the 'true' figure, the FMS average is only 56 per cent of the 'true' level.

The tentative conclusion, therefore, is that the NEDO survey casts some doubt on the FMS figures for the value of farmer's and wife's labour and that these probably err on the low side. We should keep this in mind when interpreting the FMS evidence on efficiency ratios, which will tend to be too high for the smaller farms.

Wife's manual labour

The annual reports on the Farm Management Survey *(Farm Incomes in England and Wales)* do not give separate information about how much manual work farmers' wives contribute on the farms, nor was this information sought in the enquiries leading to the Wilson Report. The item is, however, separately collected in the FMS questionnaire and we have analysed the results for 1970/71. Wives' labour was also separately investigated in the NEDO Agricultural Manpower survey of 1970.

The total contribution of wives' labour in relation to all other kinds of agricultural labour — about 5 per cent of the total in 1970/71 — may not seem to be of much importance, but, on certain sizes and types of farm, it is far from negligible and its omission would certainly affect many of the group comparisons which are being made.

Of every 100 farmers interviewed in the NEDO survey, 83 were married but only 52 had wives who did any farm work. They put in an average of 17 hours per week. The highest proportion of wives working on the farm occurred on dairy farms and the lowest on cropping farms; and wives who worked on cropping farms put in only about half as many hours per week as wives working on dairy farms, among whom one in six worked at least 30 hours a week. On small farms, more wives were working — and working longer hours — than on large farms. It is also noticeable that where the farmer was working longer hours, the wife also was helping for longer periods.

If the 'nil returns' are included — that is, allowing for the wives who did no work on the farm — the average number of hours worked was 8·8 per week, with the following distribution by type of farm:

Hours of farm work per week by farmers and wives, 1970

	Farmers	Wives	Total
Dairy	67·6	13·4	81·0
Livestock	64·9	10·2	75·1
Pigs/poultry	59·5	10·2	69·7
Cropping	58·4	5·7	64·1
Horticulture	59·8	12·8	72·6
Mixed	64·4	9·2	73·6
Total	63·8	8·8	72·6

Source: NEDO report on *Agricultural Manpower in England and Wales, 1972.*

All these features are confirmed by data taken from the FMS tape for 1970/71, though these data are in monetary terms and not in hours, the work having been valued at an hourly rate and based on earnings of paid women workers. (In the year ending 30 September 1970, the average hourly earnings of hired regular full-time women agricultural workers amounted to 28·8 p, according to the Wages and Employment Enquiry made by the MAFF.) Table 5.16 summarises the data by size of farm business (smd).

Table 5.16
Value of wife's labour, by size of business,
England and Wales, 1970/71

Size of business (smd)	All farms (excluding horticulture)			Specialist dairy			General cropping		
	£	As percentage of farmer's and wife's labour	As percentage of total labour	£	As percentage of farmer's and wife's labour	As percentage of total labour	£	As percentage of farmer's and wife's labour	As percentage of total labour
300–	87	11·0	7·6	128	16·5	12·1	41	5·1	3·3
400–	112	13·3	8·9	158	17·1	12·9	59	7·5	3·9
500–	110	13·1	7·1	143	16·1	9·4	57	7·4	3·4
600–	115	14·0	7·1	131	14·0	8·7	71	9·0	3·5
700–	101	12·6	5·2	143	15·3	7·4	53	7·3	2·6
800–	88	10·5	4·2	108	11·3	5·3	39	6·3	1·7
900–	83	10·9	3·6	141	14·5	6·4	35	6·8	1·3
1,000–	75	10·5	3·0	100	12·5	4·1	52	7·5	1·7
1,100–	84	10·7	3·1	107	13·0	3·9	52	7·0	1·8
1,200–	80	11·2	2·6	95	12·3	3·4	46	7·7	1·2
1,500–	62	9·3	1·6	70	9·3	1·9	37	6·4	0·9
1,800–	52	8·3	1·0	33	4·9	0·7	69	11·4	1·2
2,400–	46	8·8	0·7	51	8·9	0·8	55	11·7	0·8
3,000–	62	12·8	0·7	—	—	—	63	18·3	0·7
3,600–	19	6·0	0·2	—	—	—	5	2·4	—
4,200 and over	35	13·8	0·2	—	—	—	58	24·1	0·4

The table shows that the contribution of the farmer's wife to the total supply of labour reached its peak in the size-group 400–500 smd, and .that on specialist dairy farms it reached as much as 12·9 per cent of the total labour in that size-group. These would be farms of about 65 acres with about 30 cows.

The general level of the FMS figures for the value of wife's labour seems to be rather low when compared with the results of the NEDO survey. This indicated an average of 8·8 hours per week which, if valued at 28·8p per hour, would give £132 per year, whereas the FMS figures suggest an average of about £100. Moreover, this FMS figure was for the year following that in which the NEDO survey was made, so that it should probably be reduced by about 10 per cent to provide a better basis for comparison. This widens the discrepancy between the two sources. Either the FMS survey was obtaining lower estimates of the number of hours worked or those hours were being valued at less than the current average wage for women agricultural workers. This being so, it seems reasonable to conclude that the FMS has not been overstating the element of farmers' wives' labour, and may well have been understating it.

Notes

[1] Our italics.

[2] Suppose, for example, that we are considering whether the difference between an efficiency ratio of 108·9 for farms of 50–100 acres (494 farms in the sample, standard deviation 17·4) and one of 116·6 for farms of 100–150 acres (416 farms, standard deviation 18·5) is 'statistically significant', or whether the variation around each of these averages is such that a second pair of samples drawn at random from a 'population' of farms made up of both these size-groups might give rise to averages which showed as great a difference as this. We may use the formula for the standard error of the difference between two means:

$$\sigma(\overline{X}_1 - \overline{X}_2) = \sqrt{\frac{\sigma_1^2}{N_1} + \frac{\sigma_2^2}{N_2}}$$

The statistic T is the ratio:

$$\frac{\text{Difference between two means}}{\text{Standard error of difference between two means}}$$

If the value of T is greater than 1·96, there is less than one chance in 20 that the difference recorded could have occurred if the two samples had been drawn from the same population. In the case quoted

$$T = \frac{7·7}{\sqrt{0·616 + 0·824}} = \frac{7·7}{\sqrt{1·440}} = \frac{7·7}{1·2} = 6·42$$

so that the observed difference is certainly significant at the 5 per cent level of probability (p = 0·05).

Strictly speaking these tests are not fully applicable to the Farm Management Survey data, because the farms in the survey are not drawn entirely at random from the whole 'population' of farms in each size-group. However, there is a certain random element in the method of selection used, and the calculations here described are probably a fair indication of the true levels of significance which would occur between means based on a fully randomised sampling procedure.

[3] The following observations concerning the efficiency ratios of farms of different types but of the same acreage size-groups remain when due allowance is made for comparability of acreage. No other significant differences were recorded.

Size of farm (crops and grass acres)	
20–50 and 50–100	The respective efficiency ratios for dairy farms (103·8 and 111·7) was significantly higher than those for livestock farms (92·1 and 102·3)
50–100	The efficiency ratio for cropping farms (108·8) was significantly higher than for livestock farms (102·3) but not significantly lower than for dairy farms (111·7)
100–150	There was no significant difference in efficiency between dairy, livestock, cropping and mixed farms
400–500	Livestock farms (131·7) and cropping farms (125·1) had a significantly higher efficiency ratio than dairy farms (118·2), but the difference between livestock and cropping farms was not significant.

[4] See Figure 7 on p. 21 of the Zuckerman report.

[5] For a description of the method used to calculate the imputed salary see Britton, D.K. 'The analysis of net farm income: an examination of Farm Management Survey data', *Journ. of Agric. Economics,* XXI, no. 3, 1970.

[6] Gulbrandsen, O. and Lindbeck, A. *The Economics of the Agricultural Sector,* Stockholm 1973.

[7] Hjelm, L. *Economies of Size and Economies of Growth in Farming.* A paper delivered at 4th meeting of Group of Experts on Farm Rationalisation, Committee on Agricultural Problems, UN Economic Commission For Europe, Geneva 1965.

[8] *Farm Incomes in England and Wales, 1972–73,* p. 9.

[9] It is interesting to note that a recent study reports that dairy farmers in the Netherlands work about 3,000 hours a year, although the number of hours decreased by 10 per cent in the period 1963–73. Dr Boonman in a paper to Symposium on the Organisation of Production in Large-Scale Enterprises, UN Economic Commission for Europe, Committee on Agricultural Problems, Burgas, Bulgaria 1974.

6 Sources of Efficiency

A general conclusion from the consideration of the term 'efficient' undertaken in Chapter 4 was that efficient farms may be identified as those which use less resources than other farms to generate a given quantity of output. Alternatively, for a given quantity of resources they generate a greater output. This superior performance is manifested in higher efficiency ratios (output per unit of input) and, when costs of resources are expressed in monetary terms, the more efficient farms show a lower cost per unit of production.

If we are to explain the differences in efficiency between small and large farms which have been pointed out in the preceding chapter, then we must look for the advantages (and disadvantages) which stem from larger-scale production – the so-called 'economies of scale' or 'returns to scale'. Scale returns are measured by the ratio of the percentage increase in output divided by the percentage increase in input, with all the factors of production (land, machinery, labour and so forth) being increased in the same proportion. For example, if a dairy farm increased its herd size, acreage, stock of labour, machinery and buildings and all other factors of production by 10 per cent, then a return to scale would have occurred if its output increased by *more* than 10 per cent. Not only would all the above-mentioned factors have to increase by the same proportion, but so would also the managerial effort and ability of the farmer himself. This could be overcome by hiring extra farming talent, such as might be supplied by a firm of managerial consultants, but it also illustrates the unreal nature of the conditions required for pure returns to scale.

Economies of size

In practice, inputs are rarely, if ever, increased in the same proportions. Consequently the term 'economies of size' is used to describe the fall in total cost per unit of production found on larger farms. For example, an economy of size occurs when the average cost of milk production per gallon in a herd producing 60,000 gallons per year is lower than in one producing 30,000 gallons. However, the larger enterprise will not necessarily be double in all respects – perhaps much less than twice the acreage or labour is needed to produce the higher output, perhaps about twice as much concentrate feed but more than twice the number of cows. The farmer may find himself quite capable of managing the larger herd without any great increase in his own effort. If the overall effect is that the average cost is reduced, then the savings in cost caused by those inputs which increase less than proportionally with output clearly more than offset the cost of those inputs which increase *more* than proportionally with output.

Economies of size can arise either within the farming process itself, such as the better utilisation of machinery, labour or other inputs (which we call 'technical' economies), or through business dealings with other firms in its purchase of inputs or the sale of its products (covered by the term 'marketing' economies — with 'marketing' being interpreted in its broadest sense).

'Marketing' economies

Under the heading of 'marketing economies' come the discounts which can be secured for bulk purchases of fertilizer, feed and fuel, the better prices for products which arise from 'guaranteed' deliveries, cheaper sources of credit, and so forth. In their report on the *Scale of Enterprise in Farming* (1961), the Zuckerman Committee regarded such economies as difficult to measure and unlikely to be as significant in their effect as 'technical' economies. While they remain the less documented area of sources of economies, we cannot accept that they can be disregarded as irrelevant, bearing in mind the increasingly prevalent tendency to treat farms as businesses which not only have to be well organised for efficient production, but also have to make the most of every opportunity in buying and selling. This attitude has become especially strong among farmers with larger businesses, and these large farms are more likely to secure discounts and premiums simply because of their greater volume of production.[1]

Economies in the purchase of inputs

The motives behind discounts which the suppliers of farming inputs are willing to give for large orders include the reduced transport and administrative costs per unit for greater quantities, and the encouragement of a greater volume of trade on which a smaller percentage profit margin can yield a larger total profit.

Table 6.1 shows the discounts which a merchant was offering on fertilizers in south-east England in 1973. Very large purchasers could probably negotiate further small discounts or deal direct with the manufacturers. Beyond the level of 6 tons, the rate of discount did not increase very much, so the benefit gained by making a large-scale purchase rather than taking medium quantities was negligible on these figures. This scale of discount appears to discourage small orders, on which punitive surcharges are imposed. One might expect the small, non-progressive farmer with a preponderance of grass to be the most likely to order small amounts of fertilizer and hence to be at a cost disadvantage.

Table 6.1
Discount on price of fertilizer: basic price £53.20 per ton

Quantity (tons)	£	Discount (percentage of basic price)
0·2	+18 surcharge	+33·8
0·2—0·5	+12 surcharge	+22·6
0·5—1·0	+ 6 surcharge	+11·3
1—2	0	0
2—4	−1	−1·9
4—6	−1·70	−3·2
6—10	−2·70	−5·1
10—50	−2·80	−5·3
50+	−3·00	−5·6
(Additional self-haulage discount	−1·00)	(−1·9)

Source: Private correspondence.

It is interesting to note that a further discount of 1·9 per cent was being offered if the farmer collected the fertilizer from the mill himself (making the maximum discount available 7·5 per cent) and this discount was available on all quantities over one ton. Unfortunately, we have no data by which to gauge the relative abilities of large and small farms to take advantage of this transport bonus; certainly the large farm may possess its own lorry and the saving will be greater in absolute figures (£100 on 100 tons), but, on the other hand, the small farm may have surplus labour which can be used for short hauls with tractor and trailer.

Costs of borrowing

Farming must be unusual among major industries in relying so little on borrowed funds. Liabilities in agriculture are in the region of only 10 per cent of total assets.[2] Probably more than half the farms use no credit at all. However, with increasing emphasis falling on the business side of farming, the farmer's attention is often drawn to the use and costs of credit, making it is reasonable to look for possible economies of size arising here.

Only a very few farm businesses in the United Kingdom are organised as public companies with the consequent ability to raise capital by issuing shares to the public. The reason for this is that most farms are small compared with companies in other industries, and shares of small firms can be issued neither economically nor in sufficient quantity to allow a market to be established.[3] Also, historically, returns have allegedly been below the level which a company promoter might regard as adequate.[4] While most of the farms operated as public companies in British agriculture are probably large, any economies gained through the ability of this type of business to raise capital at preferential rates are of little overall significance because of their small numbers.

The major source of credit for farming is the commercial banks, which probably lend about half the total. In October 1974, bank loans to agriculture amounted to about £1,000 million, while the total borrowing by agriculture was about £2,080 million. Lending by other institutions, principally the Agricultural Mortgage Corporation (AMC) for land purchase and improvement, came to about £300 million, and credit from private sources and merchants (considered as all payments outstanding between the delivery of goods and the settlement of accounts) about £750 million. If the functions of farming and landownership are separated, commercial bank loans dominate the credit used by farming.[5]

An investigation into the availability of capital and credit to UK agriculture[6] found that bank customers were charged various rates of interest. While the typical rate charged to farmers was in the range Bank rate (later changed to Base Rate) + 2 per cent to Bank rate + 3 per cent, a low rate (Bank rate + 1½ per cent) was charged on 'blue chip' farmers' loans, such as to big farming (private) companies and estates − that is, large, creditworthy farmers in a position to offer good security if necessary. Size alone did not appear to be an important factor; preferential rates could be given for a good 'connection' and were quite often available to a farmer of any size provided the account was operated to the bank's satisfaction. Banks were also influenced favourably by the size of any credit balance held for part of the year. Higher than normal rates did not seem to be necessarily associated with small size and were used as a disciplinary weapon against farmers who exceeded the agreed credit ceiling; where a hard core of credit was building up because the farmer was persistently making losses (a situation of increasing riskiness); or in order to encourage the farmer to transfer his borrowing to other institutions, such as the AMC.

As far as bank charges outside interest were concerned, the sums involved were related to the amount of work undertaken by the bank. 'Arrangement fees' for loans and 'commitment fees' were involved only where such facilities were used, but it would appear that a 'commitment fee' for a large sum (say, if the bank arranged standby credit of £100,000 for a year) would be more likely to be charged if the credit were *not* used than on a small sum. Usually the commission on administering transactions in farm accounts was levied on a 'cost per transaction' basis, with due allowance made for any credit balances. The commission so calculated might work out at about 0·125 per cent, which would reduce to (say) 0·1 per cent on a large turnover.

Summing up, preferential charges for bank credit are available, but the large farmer is only likely to secure them if size is accompanied by greater creditworthiness. In any event, such economies are not great in absolute terms and probably of little significance when compared with the total costs of farming.

Perhaps the more important effect of size on cost of credit for farming is that the small farmer may be less able to negotiate a bank loan than a large farmer, and hence would be more likely to take credit from merchants or to enter into hire purchase agreements for machinery or livestock purchase — both more costly than bank credit. Extended merchant credit can be very costly because it usually involves loss of discount for payment within a specified period (say, a month to six weeks) which, when converted to an annual rate, can be punitive.[7] In addition, further charges may be imposed for protracted delays in payment. However, the two-way flow of goods between merchants and farmers (for example, grain from the farmer and fertilizer and animal feeds from the merchant) often makes their association very close, so that the merchant may perhaps give cheap credit to retain the farmer's goodwill and reciprocal custom. It is generally agreed that this sort of arrangement is disappearing. Hire purchase agreements are often deceptively expensive because the rate of interest quoted is usually the 'flat' rate on the sum borrowed, whereas, in reality, the monthly repayments will progressively reduce the size of the outstanding capital. For example, 9

113

per cent 'flat' rate over three years is equivalent to an effective interest rate of 17½ per cent. Obviously borrowing from commercial banks on overdraft or loan account would be considerably cheaper; the report on the availability of capital and credit, referred to earlier[6], found that hire purchase formed only 1 per cent of the borrowing of owner-occupiers but 3 per cent of that of tenants — reflecting the relative reluctance of banks to lend directly without the security of the land. Unfortunately no figures are available by which the effect of size on the composition of liabilities can be assessed, but it is suspected that the smaller farmer — and particularly the smaller tenant — is relatively more dependent on such expensive sources of credit.

Economies in the sale of products

It appears that, in the United Kingdom, the large farm has no significant advantage when it comes to securing better prices for its products solely on account of its greater volume of output. This stems from a mixture of the nature of its products, the structure of the industry, the systems of price regulation by the state and the marketing institutions that have been set up by the farmers themselves and the state. This can be illustrated by taking individually some of the major agricultural products in turn.

The prices of *cereals* which enter the UK market system are fixed by negotiation between farmer and merchant (except in the case of intervention buying) and one might expect this system to favour the large farmers. In the United States, a survey of maize growers showed that 'the larger the volume to be sold regularly, the better the potential for a higher annual average price'.[1] However, in the UK in the late 1960s it was found[8] that about one third of merchants interviewed did not vary prices between one customer and another (though prices were, of course, varied according to the quality of the grain the customer offered). Only 8 per cent of merchants varied price according to the *quantity* of grain offered (Table 6.2), hence, in this respect, an economy of size would not seem to be widely available. The extent of the price variation, where it existed, was relatively small — of the order of 2 per cent or less. It was apparent that existence of any substantial price variation soon became known among a merchant's customers and could very quickly lose him goodwill; in any case, margins in merchanting were usually too small to allow any large upward adjustments in the buying price. Because merchants who bought grain from farmers also tended to be suppliers of compound animal feeds and fertilizers, some merchants (27 per cent) allowed a small variation in grain price to farmers who purchased large amounts of these

114

inputs. This economy could equally be regarded as an additional discount on the large-scale purchase of fertilizer and feed. This two-way flow of goods is also reflected in the apparently odd situation where a farmer who has run up debts with the merchant, and therefore could be regarded as not a particularly attractive business proposition, is given preferential prices for his grain. By doing so, the merchant secures delivery of the grain and is able, if necessary, to deduct the debt before paying the farmer.

Table 6.2

Variations in grain purchase price between merchant firms and farmer customers

	Number of merchants	Percentage of sample
No variation between customers	82	32
Variation made:		
to large buyers of feed	46	18
for customer loyalty	46	18
where the customer owes money	39	15
to attract new customers	27	10
to large buyers of fertilizer	23	9
according to quantity of grain supplied	20	7
all other reasons	22	8
no definite answer	31	12
	336[1]	

[1] The sample comprised 260 merchant businesses. The 'Number of merchants' column exceeds this figure because some merchants varied prices for more than one reason.

Source: Britton, D.K., *Cereals in the United Kingdom: Production, Marketing and Utilisation*, Pergamon, 1969.

However, the large farmer can often obtain a higher price for his grain than the small farmer for another reason. The National Wheat Survey of 1964[9] found that larger growers achieved significantly higher returns per ton because they had the facilities to store grain on their farms beyond the period immediately after harvest, when prices are usually low, until a time when prices were higher. Of course, the costs of storage must be set against such gains, and any net benefit might be more properly regarded as some combination of economies of size bestowed by capital (which makes large grain stores more attractive than small stores in terms of annual cost per ton stored) and by financial size which may enable large farms to retain stocks while small farms find the need for immediate cash more pressing.

With *milk*, no price advantage can be gained simply by virtue of the volume produced; prices, which apply to almost all of the milk sold off farms, while varying with season and quality, do not directly reflect the different costs to the Milk Marketing Board of collecting small or large consignments. In practice, an apparent *diseconomy* of size exists through the price bonus which is offered to farms installing bulk milk tanks, as part of the Milk Marketing Board's policy to reduce churn collection with its inherently higher costs. The bonus is greater on small capacity tanks (increasing the 1973 price for milk by about 6 per cent with a period of two to three years over which the cost of the tank should be recouped) than on large tanks (bonus less than 2 per cent with a pay-back period of more than six years). This greater incentive to small producers must be the result of the MMB realising where its greatest potential cost savings can be made, given that it has the responsibility of collecting milk and that it does not vary its price to farmers according to volume of production.

Livestock which are sold for meat through auction markets cannot, of course, command a premium simply according to the scale of enterprise from which they come; neither can meat sold to organisations such as the Fatstock Marketing Corporation or bacon factories, where the farmer is a price-taker rather than a negotiating party. Only in those cases where the farmer and butcher directly negotiate can the price possibly vary according to volume, and these account for only a minor share of the total volume of meat. Egg and poultry-meat sales are probably more subject to price variation. It is estimated that between 30 and 40 per cent of eggs are sold by producers direct to retail shops, but firm figures are difficult to come by.

Contracting as a source of economies of size

The Committee of Inquiry on Contract Farming in the UK (chairman Sir James Barker)[10] found that in 1970/71 the advantage gained by farmers from such arrangements was primarily that of a reduced level of risk. Higher product prices or lower input costs did not appear to be of importance, although the free technical advice which often becomes available with contracts between farmers and suppliers of animal feed and fertilizers, and so forth, could be regarded as a cost-reducing item. The avoidance of market hazards could often result in producers operating a larger production unit, or specialising in a particular line; contracts could thus enable advantage to be gained from economies of size generated within the farm business, while not being themselves a direct source of economies. While written contracts between farmers and buyers for disposal of produce (excluding marketing board arrangements and forward contracts for selling cereals) only account for a small proportion of total agricultural output (about 11 per cent) involving 12 per cent of holdings in Great Britain, and only about 6 per cent of commercial holdings have procurement contracts, written contracts are much more common among large businesses than among small ones (Table 6.3). However, it is impossible to tell whether this represents an economy of size because of the intangible nature of many of the costs and benefits of contracting.

Table 6.3

Estimated percentage of holdings with written contracts by smd size category in Great Britain, 1970/71

Size of farm (smd)	Percentage of total holdings with contracts[2]
275–1,199[1]	13·1
1,200–2,399	26·7
2,400+	44·6
Total	17·5

[1]   For Scotland the smallest size category was 250–1,199 smd.

[2]   Excluding contracts for cereals, and those made with the British Sugar Corporation or the marketing boards for hops, milk, potatoes and wool. Forward sale contracts for cereals were excluded because they are made after the production phase has been completed and therefore do not impinge on production decisions.

Source: *Report of Committee of Inquiry on Contract Farming*, HMSO Cmd. 5099, 1972.

Conclusion on economies of size obtained in buying and selling

It must be remembered that, for those agricultural products which can be the subject of negotiation between producer and buyer, the farmer who has a large quantity to sell and is trying to obtain a premium above the market price is liable to be confronted by a buyer who will be attempting to get a discount for what is, to him, bulk purchase. The seller (the farmer) may be in a position to make some concession on price if there are economies in large-scale production through lower input costs or greater technical efficiency, or he may have to accept a lower price if high volume production has resulted in a generally lower quality of product.

On the whole, it would appear that 'marketing economies' in the form of reduced input costs (including cost of credit) are of small or modest proportions, with factors other than size counting strongly, although these factors (creditworthiness, loyalty in trading etc.) may often be associated with size. As regards the price of farm products, the opportunities for economies in the form of premiums appear to be severely limited in the UK; large producers of the major agricultural (as opposed to horticultural) products do not appear to benefit in price from the larger quantities they market.

In contrast, large farming businesses in the United States [11] appear to have made more use of their marketing superiority. It was observed among maize growers in the Middle West that 'large units . . . generally bypassed local market outlets. They marketed directly to a terminal or to large-volume users'. [12] In order to specialise in those commodities in which contract production has become common practice (vegetables, turkeys, potatoes, nursery and greenhouse products and cattle fattened on grain) they had to turn away from other crops like wheat, maize and soya beans. This move was made for marketing reasons, not technical ones. If contract production spreads in the United Kingdom it is only to be expected that the marketing advantages of large-scale production will have some influence on the distribution of the various kinds of livestock and crops between farm businesses of different sizes.

'Technical' economies

'Technical' economies of size are those which arise within the business itself through its more efficient use of land, labour, capital (in its variety of forms) and of the abilities of the entrepreneur — the farmer himself. These economies can be looked at from the view of what might be expected from our knowledge of factors of production, or from the view of what economies are achieved on farms in practice. Here both approaches will be used, and the MAFF Farm Management Survey will be drawn upon for data on what happens in practice.

Traditional economic theory relates economies of size to the period of time under consideration and the ability of a business to alter the quantities of resources it employs. For example, if a dairy farmer considers his management policy over, say, the next six months he may decide that certain characteristics of his farm must be accepted for what they are – it may be impossible to alter its acreage or its stock of buildings, and it may be difficult to change the size of the labour force or the number of cows. Other resources are not fixed – for example, he can vary the quantities of concentrate feed used or the amount of fertilizer used on the grassland. Naturally, the length of time under review influences which resources are fixed and which are variable. Traditional theory views each bundle of 'fixed' resources separately; each bundle can be used with a range of variable inputs to produce a range of outputs – more concentrate feed will produce more milk and greater output will utilise the capacity of the fixed resources more fully. The curve representing the average cost of production for any one scale of production is typically U-shaped; it shows that, at first, the average costs decline with increasing output because the cost of fixed inputs is spread over more units. Eventually, in the traditional textbook analysis, average costs level off and then rise as increasing proportions of variable inputs have to be added to the fixed inputs in order to increase output. For example, to increase milk yields beyond a certain level, disproportionately large quantities of extra feed have to be used. Economies of size are said to operate when an increase in the scale of enterprise (a move to a larger quantity of the inputs which are fixed in the short term) results in a fall in the lowest point of the short-run average cost curve. Beyond a certain size, the lowest points of successive short-run average cost curves may rise, and diseconomies are then said to exist. (See Figure 6.1.)

When economies of size operate, the decline in the overall level of costs will not mean that each element of the total falls. For example, it is quite possible for the average cost of medicines per gallon of milk produced to rise with increasing herd size, but this may be more than offset by the fall in housing costs, so average total costs decline.

It has been suggested [13] that it would be more realistic to describe resources as 'discrete' or 'divisible' rather than 'fixed' or 'variable'. Divisible resources are those available in measured quantities, for example, fertilizers, while discrete resources are available to the farm business only in counted quantities (whole numbers) of specific size units, for example, tractors. Each U-shaped curve would then apply to a collection of discrete resources, for example, one comprising two men plus one tractor plus a milking parlour and fifty cows. However, as many of the discrete resources are also those that are traditionally regarded as fixed in the short term, the implications of using either classification are similar.

119

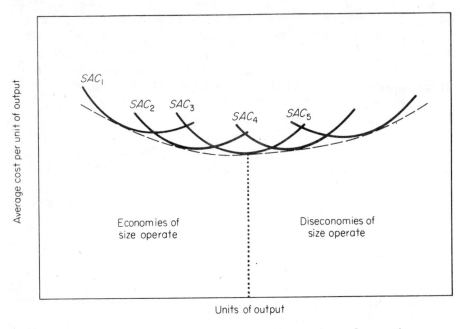

Fig. 6.1   Average costs of production at different sizes of operation

SAC_1, SAC_2 etc. represent the short-run average cost curves at different levels of herd size.

Revealed sources of economies of size

The published reports from the Farm Management Survey are capable of yielding information on the practical manifestations of the sources of economies, although manipulation of the data is necessary. Supporting evidence is provided by a wide range of other published studies, both from the United Kingdom and abroad, although many of these concentrate on economies of size associated with single inputs, such as labour, and neglect the simultaneous diseconomies experienced with other inputs.

First, a point related to the theory of economies of size must be clarified. When such economies are discussed, or graphs are drawn to illustrate them, quantity of output is the conventional measure of size to use (see Figure 6.1). However, farm size is not usually measured in terms of quantity of output — this is made almost impossible in practice because of the heterogeneous nature of the output of most farms. (Exceptions might be egg production or milk production on specialist holdings.) Certainly, comprehensive statistics using output, whether physical or expressed in monetary terms, as the measure of size are not published in

120

the United Kingdom. The two most commonly used measures are based on single inputs – acreage or standard labour requirements (smd's). The relative merits of these as measures of size are discussed in Chapter 3. However, as smd's and the gross output of farms are quite closely related, smd's can be used as an acceptable proxy for the (value of) farm output, and economies associated with larger smd size-groups can be reasonably taken as economies of size, defined more conventionally.

Table 6.4 shows the breakdown of average costs used to produce £100 worth of gross output in 1971/72, classified by type and size of business. These costs have been derived from published FMS data. Of course, the figures shown for each size-group are only averages, and there would be considerable variation between farms in each group. There is also no reason to suppose that each farm is operating at the lowest part of its average cost curve. [14] However, given these important reservations, the figures can be taken as a broad indication of the resources used by different sizes of business.

The total cost of inputs to achieve £100 of gross output is of course the obverse of the measure of efficiency used elsewhere (value of output per £100 input), and the comments on size and efficiency made in Chapter 5 are equally applicable here. The total cost of inputs per £100 output can be interpreted as the average cost of production, and the most striking feature of this column in Table 6.4 is the decline in total costs which occurs when moving from the smallest size of business (275–599 smd's). However, as this improvement in efficiency has already been discussed in detail in Chapter 5, the purpose here is to examine the way individual cost items, which change with business size, contribute to this overall effect. If the cost of any input per £100 gross output falls as business size increases we may interpret this fall as an economy of size in the use of that input.

Fixed capital as a source of economies of size

Fixed capital, in this context, is taken to include all the plant and machinery, buildings and equipment on farms. It is not all used (or worn out) in one year, unlike the 'circulating', 'working' or 'variable' capital such as fertilizers, feed, seed and so forth. Lower purchase costs and/or operating costs per unit of capacity are often given as a major source of economies of size in the use of capital. For example, in Table 6.5 it can be seen that the cost per milking unit of new milking parlours falls steadily with increasing size of parlour. Assuming that the effective working lives of all sizes of parlour are the same, and that maintenance costs form a fixed proportion of initial outlay, then the annual cost per milking unit

Table 6.4

Average costs (£) to produce £100 of gross output, 1971/72

Farm type and size / Size-group (smd)	Mean smd	Gross output	Total input	Rent and rates	Farmer and wife labour	Paid labour	Unpaid labour	Total labour	Machinery and power	Feed	Fertilizer and seed	Feed, fertilizer and seed	Other costs	Total inputs less farmer and wife labour
Specialist dairy														
275–599	451	100	78·78	5·30	15·25	4·42	1·76	21·43	12·01	27·45	4·49	31·94	8·10	63·54
600–1,199	873	100	75·09	5·90	7·65	8·39	1·33	17·37	10·98	26·97	6·11	33·08	7·76	67·34
1,200–1,799	1,444	100	70·94	6·73	3·78	10·98	1·27	16·03	10·90	23·11	6·52	29·63	7·65	67·16
1,800–2,399	2,028	100	74·52	7·33	2·58	12·65	0·46	15·69	11·93	23·38	8·05	31·43	8·14	71·94
2,400+	2,824	100	75·10	7·41	1·01	14·05	0·44	15·50	10·42	24·85	8·00	32·85	8·92	74·09
Mainly dairy														
275–599	479	100	80·16	5·77	14·26	5·61	2·61	22·48	11·74	28·02	4·80	32·82	7·35	65·90
600–1,199	863	100	73·78	6·34	7·41	7·79	1·90	17·10	11·76	24·45	6·48	30·93	7·65	66·36
1,200–1,799	1,464	100	75·78	7·32	3·91	11·53	1·46	16·90	11·88	23·78	7·88	31·66	8·02	71·86
1,800–2,399	2,104	100	74·80	8·66	1·99	15·33	0·94	18·26	12·81	17·56	9·79	27·35	7·72	72·81
2,400+	3,119	100	76·53	8·39	1·25	15·90	0·36	17·51	12·32	21·19	9·35	30·54	7·77	75·28
Livestock, cattle and sheep														
275–599	442	100	79·22	8·82	16·01	5·19	2·99	24·19	14·74	15·85	6·76	22·61	8·86	63·21
600–1,199	865	100	71·01	10·10	8·18	8·87	2·78	19·83	13·32	11·62	8·18	19·80	7·96	62·83
1,200–1,799	1,449	100	68·17	10·00	4·45	11·25	1·98	17·68	13·05	12·39	8·28	20·67	6·77	63·72
1,800–2,399	2,042	100	68·10	8·89	3·02	10·87	2·01	15·90	12·68	12·91	8·72	21·63	9·00	65·08
2,400+	2,875	100	67·90	10·77	1·84	14·72	0·24	16·80	13·00	9·02	10·07	19·09	8·24	66·06

Table 6.4 continued

Farm type and size / Size-group (smd)	Mean smd	Gross output	Total input	Rent and rates	Farmer and wife labour	Paid labour	Unpaid labour	Total labour	Machinery and power	Feed	Fertilizer and seed	Feed, fertilizer and seed	Other costs	Total inputs less farmer and wife labour
Cropping (mainly cereals)														
275–599	445	100	84.30	11.99	9.98	10.37	2.04	22.39	19.70	7.47	14.14	21.61	8.61	74.32
600–1,199	884	100	77.02	13.14	3.78	12.64	0.79	17.21	18.17	5.76	14.42	20.18	8.32	73.24
1,200–1,799	1,432	100	75.79	12.60	2.02	13.94	0.85	16.81	16.33	8.47	13.31	21.78	8.27	73.77
1,800–2,399	2,060	100	74.95	13.37	1.71	16.03	0.50	18.24	15.42	6.78	13.92	20.70	7.22	73.24
2,400+	2,991	100	72.70	12.46	0.59	15.65	0.45	16.69	16.12	5.55	14.36	19.91	7.52	72.11
General cropping														
275–599	457	100	83.85	9.53	13.22	11.95	1.92	27.09	16.87	8.38	12.91	21.29	9.07	70.63
600–1,199	888	100	79.39	9.40	5.82	13.94	1.47	21.23	16.59	11.36	11.89	23.25	8.92	73.57
1,200–1,799	1,499	100	78.98	9.64	2.74	16.80	0.58	20.12	16.13	11.51	12.53	24.04	9.05	76.24
1,800–2,399	2,122	100	79.74	9.71	1.96	17.38	0.84	20.18	15.51	12.42	13.32	25.74	8.60	77.78
2,400+	3,144	100	78.49	9.76	0.93	19.85	0.48	21.26	16.07	8.78	13.11	21.89	9.51	77.56
Mixed														
275–599	402	100	87.42	7.63	14.22	2.38	8.51	25.11	13.68	27.22	6.80	34.02	6.99	73.21
600–1,199	897	100	79.64	7.14	6.78	12.81	1.50	21.09	12.70	22.45	8.65	31.10	7.61	72.86
1,200–1,799	1,521	100	76.41	8.01	3.63	10.88	2.64	17.15	13.58	21.81	8.93	30.74	6.93	72.78
1,800–2,399	2,118	100	79.47	8.43	2.01	13.66	0.81	16.48	12.55	26.89	8.19	35.08	6.93	77.46
2,400+	3,038	100	79.87	8.27	1.01	16.45	0.35	17.81	12.63	25.17	8.85	34.02	7.14	78.86

Table 6.5
Costs of herringbone milking parlours, 1972

Size (number of cows)	Price (£)	Cost per cow place (£)
8	2,400	300
10	2,850	285
12	3,200	267
16	3,850	240
20	4,600	230

Source: Nix J. *Farm Management Pocketbook,* 5th edition, Wye College, University of London, 1972.

Table 6.6
Costs of bulk milk tanks, 1973

Size of tank (gallons)	Price (£)	Cost per 100 gallons storage (£)
60	650	1,083
100	850	850
150	980	653
175	1,200	686
240	1,400	583
300	1,500	500
340	1,570	462
400	1,700	425
500	2,100	420
600	2,300	383
750	3,200	427

Source: Private correspondence with Milk Marketing Board. It is understood that the prices quoted are averages based on several manufacturers.

will also fall with increasing size. Another example is given by bulk milk tanks (Table 6.6) where new cost per 100 gallons capacity generally falls with increasing size, except for the largest size of tank where small-volume manufacture makes them relatively expensive.

Table 6.7

Standard costs for farm buildings

A   Totally enclosed traditional construction general purpose building, excluding floor (a range of 8–12ft to 16ft to eaves)

Area (sq. ft)	Cost per sq. ft
1,000	£1·25 to £1·75
3,000	£1·00 to £1·30
5,000	£0·90 to £1·15

B   Open-fronted building (traditional construction – excluding floor)

Area (sq. ft)	Cost per sq. ft
1,000	90p
2,000	80p
3,000	75p

Source: Nix, J. *Farm Management Pocketbook* 5th edition, Wye College, University of London, 1972.
Standard costs are revised periodically, and so figures quoted must not be taken as currently applying. They are based on the cost of labour and new materials used for construction, excluding overheads and profits. The latter are very variable but on average building firms would add about one-third to cover them.

A further example is provided by grain storage (see Figure 6.2) where cost per ton stored falls rapidly at first and then more slowly as storage capacity rises; this applies to floor storage, bin storage and also sealed silo storage. The purchase price of general farm buildings exhibits the same economies of size. Table 6.7 shows examples of approximate standard costs as calculated for the Farm Capital Grant Scheme (as from May 1972) where the farmer chooses this basis for the award of state grant instead of actual costs.

The cost of operating machinery arises not only from its initial purchase but also from its operation – fuel, repairs and maintenance and so forth. Table 6.8 shows the theoretical annual costs of operating wheeled tractors of different sizes. It is assumed that each machine is operated for 1,000 hours each year, and that each is traded in or sold after six years for a quarter of its original cost. In terms of cost per horsepower per year the figures show that economies are achieved with increasing tractor size

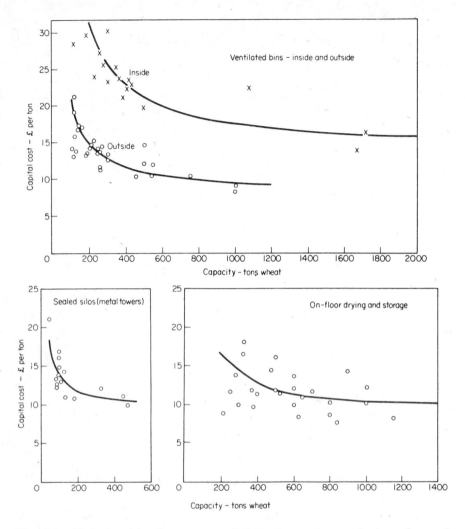

Fig. 6.2 Relationship between capital cost per ton and size of cereal store

Source: Britton, D.K. *Cereals in the United Kingdom: production, marketing and utilisation,* Pergamon, 1969, based on data supplied by the trade.

except for the largest size of tractor; these are relatively expensive when new, probably because relatively few are manufactured. However, if the tractor driver is regarded as an integral part of operating the machine, and his wages are included in the running costs, then the largest machine becomes the cheapest in terms of cost per horsepower per year because the man's labour charge is spread over a much greater horsepower. This applies whether labour is charged for only the 1,000 hours notionally worked or for the full man-year. Economies of size will only be gained if the available power is utilised; if the largest tractor is worked only at the same power as the smallest, the cost per horsepower)with 1,000 hours of labour) is almost 60 per cent greater, and over 150 per cent greater if labour is excluded. The larger capacity of powerful tractors must be exploited if they are to be as cheap or cheaper to operate than smaller tractors.

Table 6.8
Tractor costs

	Size of tractor			
	35–40 h.p.	43–48 h.p.	55–65 h.p.	100 h.p.
Initial price (£)	1,250	1,400	1,650	3,100
Cost per h.p. (£)	33·33	30·77	27·5	31·00
Cost per h.p. per year (£)				
Depreciation	4·16	3·85	3·43	3·87
Tax and insurance	0·35	0·31	0·31	0·24
Repairs and maintenance	2·67	2·46	2·20	2·48
Fuel and oil	1·47	1·43	1·42	1·75
Total (excluding labour)	8·64	8·04	7·35	8·34
Labour (1,000 hrs of labour at 54p/hr)	14·40	11·87	9·00	5·40
Total (including 1,000 hours labour)	23·04	19·91	16·35	13·74
Total (including one full man-year of labour at £1,285)	42·91	36·28	28·77	21·19

Source: Derived from Nix, J. *Farm Management Pocketbook,* 5th Edition, Wye College, University of London, 1972.

The importance of capacity utilisation is also neatly illustrated by the combine-harvester. Figure 6.3 shows the fixed costs (excluding labour) in pounds per acre associated with combines of different acreage capacities. It clearly shows that lowest costs are achieved when machines are used· at or close to full capacity, and that a small machine used at full capacity has lower fixed costs per acre than a larger machine less fully utilised. However, it may well be that farmers are willing to bear higher costs if this brings with it the consolation of sufficient spare capacity to accommodate adverse weather or breakdowns.

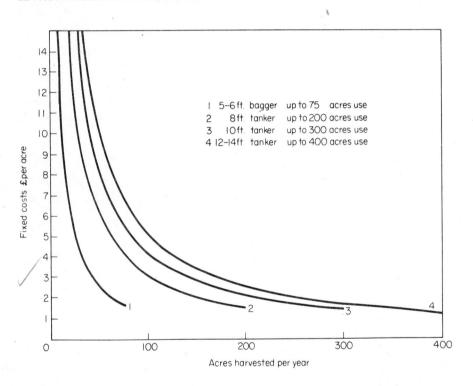

Fig. 6.3   Relationship between combine fixed costs and acreage harvested

Source: Davidson, J.G., *Farm Planning Data 1967*, Farm Economics Branch, University of Cambridge, pp. 68—9.

It appears, then, that there are good reasons to believe that from a theoretical standpoint considerable economies of size exist with items of fixed capital. Thus large farms which use large tractors, machines, buildings etc. at levels approaching full capacity should be able to enjoy lower costs per unit of production than small farms — or at least lower costs arising from the use of fixed capital. In addition, they may be able to justify equipment (such as tile drain-laying machines or grass-drying plant) for which a smaller farm would have to hire an outside contractor, at considerably greater cost per unit of work. However, data collected in the FMS fail to show that the theoretically possible economies are substantially realised in practice.

The FMS found that, in 1971/72, the value of machinery on cropping (mainly cereals) farms, mixed farms and livestock (cattle and sheep) farms increased less than proportionally with business size (measured in smd) (see Table 6.9). The foregoing discussion would suggest that machinery provided an opportunity for economies of size on these types of farm. On specialist dairy and general cropping farms, no trend was evident, while on mainly dairy farms the value of machinery increased more than proportionally with size of business, indicating a possible diseconomy of size. Care must be taken in interpreting these data, because it has been suggested that large farms tend to buy new (and hence more valuable) machinery whereas small farms tend to buy secondhand. Valuation would thus tend to overstate the physical productive capacity available on large farms and understate it on smaller ones. [15] Consequently, economies could be hidden by valuation differences on those types where none are apparent, and understated on those where economies were evident.

Because plant and machinery is not worn out in one year it is depreciated in farm accounts, conventionally by the 'diminishing balance' method. Machinery on large and small farms is treated alike, and this could produce an overestimate of depreciation on small farms where machinery might be expected to last longer because of the lower percentage of capacity at which it is worked. If this were true, an adjustment would tend to erode any economies which the data might initially suggest on large farms. However, depreciation is only one element in the total annual cost of operating machinery, and the FMS shows, in addition, data on repairs, fuels, tax and insurance, and contracting services ('hired mechanisation'). Table 6.4 shows the total costs of machinery and power to produce £100 gross output, and it can be seen that no striking economies of size are evident except with cropping (mainly cereals) where a modest fall is experienced between the small and medium sized businesses. As tractors and combines are often cited when possible economies of size are discussed, the identification of modest economies in the 'simple' farming system of mainly cereal cropping farms, where costs of machinery and power form a higher percentage of total costs than in other farming types, is not really surprising.

129

Table 6.9
Machinery stocks on farms, 1971/72

Farm type and size (smd)	Average size of business (smd)	Valuation (£) per farm	Valuation/smd (£)
Specialist dairy			
275–599	451	1,430	3·2
600–1,199	873	2,953	3·4
1,200–1,799	1,444	4,797	3·3
1,800–2,399	2,028	7,575	3·7
2,400+	2,824	8,705	3·1
Mainly dairy			
275–599	479	1,354	2·8
600–1,199	863	2,867	3·3
1,200–1,799	1,464	5,068	3·5
1,800–2,399	2,104	8,044	3·8
2,400+	3,119	12,514	4·0
Livestock (cattle and sheep)			
275–599	442	1,605	3·6
600–1,199	865	2,891	3·3
1,200–1,799	1,449	4,705	3·2
1,800–2,399	2,042	5,052	2·5
2,400+	2,875	8,397	2·9
Cropping (mainly cereals)			
275–599	445	3,428	7·7
600–1,199	884	5,958	6·7
1,200–1,799	1,432	8,059	5·6
1,800–2,399	2,060	10,945	5·3
2,400+	2,991	14,242	4·8
General cropping			
276–599	457	1,780	3·9
600–1,199	880	4,325	4·9
1,200–1,799	1,499	6,462	4·3
1,800–2,399	2,122	9,150	4·3
2,400+	3,144	12,378	3·9
Mixed			
275–599	402	1,956	4·9
600–1,199	897	3,886	4·3
1,200–1,799	1,521	5,630	3·7
1,800–2,399	2,118	7,619	3·6

Source: Derived from FMS data.

A further explanation of why economy of size in the use of machinery is not generally evident is the spatial distribution of large farms. Work in the USA [16] found, by comparing the acreage with which farm machinery was theoretically capable of coping with actual farm acreage, that large farms in the Imperial Valley of California appeared to possess an excess of machinery. However, this excess could be drastically reduced by making allowances for the time used in moving machinery between the separate blocks of land constituting the large farms. While no similar calculations appear to have been published for the UK, farms which have grown by absorbing other, non-contiguous, holdings must face this spatial problem of fragmentation, and the lack of a ring-fence must impose some additional costs to offset the potential economies of size from mechanisation, although the magnitude of this cost is not yet quantified.

Variable capital and land as sources of economies of size

The phenomenon of diminishing marginal returns in the relationship between feed and animal production (particularly yields from dairy cows) and in the relationship between fertilizer usage and crop yield is too well recognised to need further comment here, save to point out that diminishing returns, and the associated higher costs of producing high yields, occur at all scales of production. In theoretical models, diminishing returns are responsible for the eventual increase in average costs of production because the increasing cost of variable inputs more than offsets any fall in costs caused by spreading fixed costs over greater levels of output. However, it is here that marketing economies of size in reducing the costs of fertilizer and so forth will be felt.

Data from the FMS (Table 6.4) show that, in practice, large businesses on average appear to use neither more nor less 'variable capital' per unit of output than small businesses. ('Variable capital' is taken here to consist of fertilizer, seed and bought feedstuffs, as shown in the last column of Table 6.4.) It is also largely synonymous with the concept of 'divisible' resources used earlier.[17]

Economies of size in land use might arise if an increase in output required a less-than-proportional increase in acreage. This would occur where a dairy or livestock farm increased its output principally by intensification, but would be more difficult on a cropping farm. One might then expect that, all other things being equal, the cost of hiring land per unit of output would decline with increasing business size. Table 6.4 shows that this does not occur in practice; rather there appears to be some *increase* in the rent and rates element of costs in the larger dairy and livestock

131

businesses, suggesting that *diseconomies* are associated with size. On cropping farms, the rent and rates cost is relatively stable, suggesting constant returns to size.

Rent and rate costs per £100 of gross output are determined by the level of gross output per acre and the rent and rates charged per acre. Small businesses (of 275–599 smd) tend to use their land less intensively than larger businesses, as measured in gross output per acre, but their rent and rates per acre also tend to be low. [18] It would be wrong, however, to jump to the conclusion that small businesses tend to possess poor-quality land. Many factors other than land quality help determine rents – for example, a farmer might be willing to pay a high rent for land to add to his existing acreage if he could work the enlarged acreage without any additional labour or machinery, or a landlord may be content with a low rent if the tenant is near retirement or undertakes building maintenance beyond his contractual responsibility. Also it must be recalled that the FMS treats all farms as tenanted, imputing rents for owner-occupiers, and this introduces an arbitrary element into this component of total costs. On balance, and taking into account the reliability of the FMS's rent and rates figures, the results suggest that economies in the use of land do not contribute to economies of size, while on dairy farms diseconomies are evident.

Labour and management as a source of economies of size

Realised economies in the use of land or capital have been shown to be either non-existent or of an insufficient magnitude to explain the marked difference in overall efficiency which is evident between the small and medium sizes of farm business. By a process of elimination the key must lie in the economies of size shown by labour and management.

With increasing size of farm business, one might expect economies in the use of labour to arise from (1) specialisation, involving the teaching and acquisition of skills and the employment of people with special aptitudes and abilities (such as dairy cowmen or high-grade management) and (2) more capitalisation (for example the output of a man operating a large capacity machine is greater than one operating a similar but smaller capacity machine). This latter economy is self-evident, with many cases arising, such as powerful tractors, large combines; indeed, mechanisation of almost all sorts, even buildings, for one man can probably oversee a greater number of cattle if they are housed during the winter, than if they were loose in fields. The advantages that arise from specialisation, while also fairly obvious, are not supported by much experimental evidence (for example, the number of acres ploughed per day by a specialist tractor-driver as opposed to a general labourer). On the other hand, there is evidence [19] that the proportion of workers who could be described as 'specialists' is much higher on larger farms. If specialisation occurs, it could be argued that it is because such differentiation of tasks endows some benefits.

It seems that some of the diseconomies of size associated with labour in other industries do not play an important role in farming. Among these are the increased boredom associated with extremes of mechanisation and specialisation and the lack of motivation caused by isolation from other workers and from the decision-makers of the business, which result in a lower output per worker and rising absenteeism. These diseconomies probably fail to appear because, firstly, the farmer and members of his family constitute a significant proportion of the total labour force on many farms, particularly on the smaller ones, and, secondly, because very few farms are sufficiently large or organised in such a way as to preclude personal contact between workers and management. This point is more fully discussed in Chapter 5 and its Appendix 2. Ingham [20] has suggested that, in an industrial setting, a labour force of up to thirty members can operate as a 'primary group' where each member makes contact with every other member. In 1973, only 15 per cent of regular agricultural workers in England and Wales were on holdings employing 20 or more people. Ruth Gasson [21] suggests that the division of labour is far less advanced in most farming systems than in other industrial organisations, so farm workers stand to gain more satisfaction than others through exercising control over processes and events and through the variety of occupation inherent in the nature of farming.

The FMS data given in Table 6.4 show that labour is indeed the key to explaining the economies of size observable in farming. Large labour economies are experienced when moving from the smallest to the next size of business. In some cases, the fall in total inputs per £100 gross output is less than the fall in labour input (general cropping farms and specialist dairy farms), indicating diseconomies of size in the other inputs combined, while, in the other types of farming, the fall in total inputs is greater than the fall in labour input, indicating an economy of size in the other inputs, in addition to that achieved with labour, although the economy in labour input contributes, in all cases, more than half the fall in total inputs.[22]

Movements in the individual components of 'total labour' are even more illuminating. The three components are hired labour, unpaid family labour, and the labour of the farmer and his wife. As the size of business increases, the labour of the farmer and his family naturally declines as a percentage of the total workforce (see Figure 5.16), and this is reflected by a rise in the paid-labour input per £100 gross output. This must not be interpreted as a diseconomy of size in the use of labour as a whole, as it is counteracted by a decline in the other two components. The cost of unpaid family labour (other than the farmer and his wife) per £100 gross output declines with business size, although it always forms a very minor part of the total labour resource [23] and this contribution diminishes with size.

The dramatic decline with business size in the costs attributed to the labour of farmer and wife in producing £100 of gross output is the most significant feature of the labour element of costs. When moving from the smallest size of business to the next, the value attributed to the farmer's and wife's labour approximately halves, and this decline in costs (in the range £6-8) is sufficient to more than offset the increase in paid labour, producing a fall in total labour input per £100 output (even after taking into account unpaid family labour). Although the farmer and wife labour element continues to decline with larger sized businesses, it is more closely matched by increases in paid labour costs, so that total labour costs per £100 output beyond the 500–1,199 smd size of business decline little or not at all.

As has been mentioned above, on most types of farm, the only notable economies of size are achieved by labour and are evident between the smallest category of farm business (275–599 smd) and the next smallest (600–1,199 smd). The source of these economies can now clearly be seen as the labour input of the farmer and wife — in other words, the diseconomy of small size is caused by the relatively large cost attributable to the labour of farmer and wife in small businesses.

Because, on a one-man farm, the same person may have to milk cows and tend animals, drive a tractor and cultivate crops, and undertake office-work, this diseconomy may be the result of the lack of opportunity for the specialisation of labour in small businesses. No doubt an element of this type of diseconomy exists, but the real explanation is likely to lie in the area of the utilisation of capacity — the capacity of the farmer's and his wife's own labour — which is available.

Explanation of the economy of size in the use of the farmer's and wife's labour

A classification of factors of production was discussed earlier that recognised two groups — discrete (which could only be obtained in whole numbers of specific size units) and divisible (which could be used in measured quantities). The farmer is a prime example of a discrete input in that, although part-time farmers could be counted as fractions, once he is fully committed, this input cannot be subdivided. It is quite conceivable that, on a small one-man farm, the available work does not fully occupy the man, at least according to average labour requirements. On a farm with one hired man in addition to the farmer, the work may be too much for one man yet insufficient to occupy two on a regular full-time basis. Because the farmer's own labour contributes all or a major proportion of the total labour available, this under-utilisation of available labour is reflected in the relatively large labour costs attributable to the farmer if his labour is costed at the rates payable to hired workers.

Some idea of the extent of this labour surplus, or underemployment, can be gained by comparing annual expenditure on labour (including notional payments to the farmer and wife), as shown by the FMS, with the theoretical labour requirements as indicated by smd (see Chapter 3). This has been done for 1970/71 and is presented in an index form in Table 6.10 giving the 'best' group (in this case the group 1,100–1,799 smd) the value of 100 as a basis for comparison. (Note that the size-groups

Table 6.10
Indices of labour utilisation
relative to smd labour requirement, 1970/71

Type of farming	100–499	500–799	800–1,099	1,100–1,799	1,800 and over
			Indices (1,100–1,799 smd group = 100)		
Specialist dairy	134	117	106	100	107
Mainly dairy	150	104	98	100	107
Livestock (cattle and sheep)	161	118	113	100	100
Cropping (mainly cereals)	143	121	101	100	93
General cropping	138	111	105	100	93
Mixed	141	133	123	100	112
All types (excluding horticulture)	142	114	103	100	104

Derivation:
(a) a table of total labour expenditure (including farmer and wife) per smd was constructed;
(b) the expenditures were expressed with respect to that of the 1,100–1,799 size-group.

differ from those used in other tables.) The smallest businesses (100–499 smd) used much more than their 'basic' labour requirement, exceeding estimates suggested by the 'best' group by between a third and almost two-thirds. Businesses of 500–799 smd used less 'excess' labour – up to 33 per cent. It could be argued that this 'excess' labour usage was counter-balanced by reduced mechanisation, but we have already established that the lower level of mechanisation which might be expected if small farms were to compensate for higher labour usage does not, in fact, occur. Thus real underemployment of available labour appears to exist on the smallest businesses of each farming type.

Conclusion on the technical economies of size

The conclusions to be drawn from examining FMS data must be that:

1   Economies of size are available, but are principally manifested when comparison is made between the smallest size of business (275–599 smd) and the next (600–1,199 smd).

2   The major source of economies of size is the greater spreading of the cost of the labour of the farmer and wife over a larger volume of output.

3   Small businesses are associated with labour 'surpluses' or relative underemployment in that the amount of time spent per acre of crops or per head of livestock is generous by the standards of medium-sized businesses.

A comparison with the findings of the Zuckerman Committee of the 1950s

The conclusions reached on the principal sources of economies of size for 1971/72 bear a close relationship to those of the Zuckerman report of the mid-1950s; it was then concluded that the major source of economies of size was the ability of the large farm to spread its 'overhead' costs, and in particular the value of the farmer's own labour, over a greater volume of output.

Working not with the national FMS sample but with two smaller samples from Wales and East Anglia for the years 1954/55 and 1955/56, the Zuckerman Committee found that the contribution of the farmer's own labour per £100 of output declined with increasing farm size. The Zuckerman report called this 'probably the most significant feature brought out by the analysis', and this is equally true of the more recent data. Total labour input did not show as marked an initial decline with size as in 1971/72, indicating that hired labour [24] was used almost to counteract the decline in available farmer and wife labour per unit of output, as size increased. The greater decline in 1971 could be explained by an improvement in labour productivity over the intervening period coupled with the irreducible nature of the quantity of labour which the farmer himself represented, but caution must be exercised in drawing conclusions because of the differences in size criteria employed, and the smallness and heterogeneity of the Zuckerman Committee's sub-samples. However, these differences are unlikely to detract significantly from the striking similarity in the situation relating to the labour of the farmer himself.

Although, as in 1971/72, the Zuckerman Committee did not find economies of size arising from machinery (total machinery costs[25] per £100 of output was remarkably constant throughout the range of farm sizes), in the components of 'divisible' capital economies and diseconomies were identified which are not apparent for 1971/72; the cost of feedstuffs per £100 output fell steeply as farm size, measured in acres, increased. This was at least partly explained by the fact that larger farms grew more of their own feedstuffs. However, in neither the Welsh nor the East Anglian samples were farms classified by type, so changes in the proportion of output contributed by livestock form another source of explanation. Such changes with size were probably greater in East Anglia than in Wales. In both samples, nearly double the amount of fertilizer was used to produce £100 of output in the largest size-groups, as compared with the smaller. Farms of small acreage, however, had proportionately more farmyard manure available, and this may have accounted for some part of the difference, together with changes in enterprise mix. In general, the Zuckerman Committee found that the smallest farms experienced considerable diseconomies of feedstuffs-plus-fertilizer, but the sample included some small farms, the equivalents of which were excluded from the 1971/72 analysis because they were not full-time holdings. The 1971/72 data did not reveal any marked diseconomy of small size with 'divisible' capital, but, because of the non-comparability of the data from the mid-1950s and 1971/72 it is impossible to assess the extent to which any real improvement in the use of 'divisible' capital on small farms has taken place.

Evidence from other studies in the United Kingdom and abroad

While it is not feasible in a book of this sort to attempt an exhaustive review of all the published evidence on the subject of the sources of economies of size, an indication of some of the existing material will show that our conclusions, drawn from recent FMS data, are borne out by other UK studies. Furthermore, they are supported by evidence from other countries with reasonably similar agricultural systems. We are primarily concerned with the level of efficiency and sources of economies of size of whole farm businesses, and the supporting evidence we are about to quote also takes this whole farm approach. However, there also exists a body of supplementary information about the performance of single enterprises of different sizes; such studies usually necessitate some rather arbitrary cost allocations and provide only partial indicators of economies of size of farm business, as an indicated economy may be offset or augmented by economies or diseconomies elsewhere in the business. Despite these limitations on the value of enterprise studies for our present purpose, there is a good deal of impressive evidence available from such studies and we have assembled and commented upon data relating to two major enterprises – production of milk and of cereals – in an appendix (p. 148).

In many countries, labour, particularly that of the farmer himself, appears to be the major source of the diseconomy suffered by small farms, producing underemployment and low output per man. Figures for the Irish Republic illustrate the problem well. [26] Comparisons between the amount of labour actually engaged in agriculture and the amount theoretically required on the basis of average standards per animal or per acre show that underemployment was much worse on the small farms than on the larger farms (see Table 6.11). This is not seriously undermined by criticisms of the absolute levels of the figures.

The importance of this labour surplus is emphasised in the already mentioned report on farm productivity in Great Britain published in 1973 by the Economic Development Committee for Agriculture. [27] From a sample of 133 farms, it was found that the estimated labour surplus bore a statistically highly significant inverse relationship with the ratio of gross output to gross input (which the report called 'productivity' and which we call 'efficiency'). It found the surplus most acute on family farms (that is, farms where the family constituted at least 60 per cent of the labour force) which were often unable to fully utilise the family labour available. When family farms were excluded from the analysis, surplus labour was no longer such a dominant factor. Both this evidence and that from Ireland is in line with the inference drawn by us from the FMS for England and Wales.

Labour underemployment on small farms is reflected in the relatively high labour inputs needed to achieve £100 of output. Alternatively, it can appear in the reciprocal form of a low value of output from a given

138

Table 6.11
Level of underemployment of labour on farms in Ireland

Size of holding (acres)	Ratio of labour available to labour required (labour required = 100)
1–5	256
5–10	278
10–15	270
15–30	226
30–50	183
50–100	142
100–150	120
150–200	111
200–300	105
300+	115

Source: *Report of the Inter-Departmental Committee on the Problem of Small Western Farms,* Stationery Office, Dublin (Pr. 6540), 1962.

quantity of labour, economies of size being implied by a rise in output per unit of labour with increasing size of business. Some data in this form can be taken from the Netherlands. At regular intervals over the period 1948–63 studies were made by the Landbouw-Economisch Instituut of the average output performance per unit of labour on small farms in the sandy regions of the Netherlands. [28] For the years 1948, 1952, 1957 and 1963, calculations were made for different size-groups, sizes being measured in hectares. Labour performance was measured in terms of 'standard hours per labour unit'. A summary of the figures is given in Table 6.12 and Figure 6.4.

'Standard hours' are similar to the standard man-days used in the United Kingdom, except that the standard labour requirements remained unchanged from 1948 to 1963 — that is, consecutive studies were all based on the levels of efficiency and mechanisation which prevailed on reasonably well-managed farms in 1948, when 3,000 standard hours per labour unit was considered a 'normal level'. 'Labour units' represent the numbers of full-time adult male workers, other categories of workers being converted to equivalents of these units by reference to relative wages and to the amount of time spent working on the farm in the course of the year. The farmer and members of his family are included in the calculation.

Table 6.12
Labour performance on small farms in
Netherlands sandy soil regions

Size-group (hectares)	Average number of hectares (1,957)	Labour performance in standard hours per labour unit			
		1948	1952	1957	1963
1–3	2·2	1,158	1,678	2,044	2,548
3–5	4·1	1,674	2,094	2,509	2,963
5–7	5·9	1,955	2,356	3,037	3,206
7–10	8·4	2,300	2,723	3,351	3,818
10–12	10·9	2,420	2,984	3,524	4,622
12–15	13·3	2,492	3,066	3,805	4,685
15–20	17·0	2,762	3,246	4,214	4,972
20–30	23·8	3,043	3,456	4,619	5,234
over 30	42·6	3,528	3,925	4,929	6,703

Source: Landbouw-Economisch Instituut, The Hague.

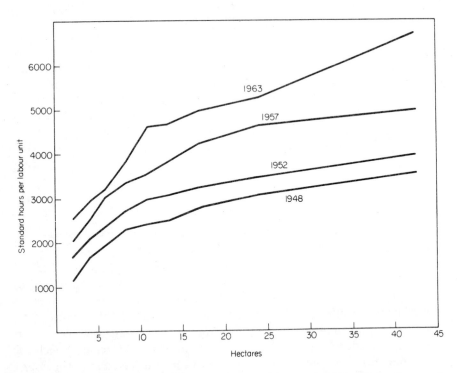

Fig. 6.4   Size of farm and labour performance, small farms in the sandy
soil regions, Netherlands, 1948, 1952, 1957 and 1963

In view of the assumption of constant 'standard hours' for performing the work connected with the crops and livestock on these farms, it is not surprising that the performance in terms of standard hours per labour unit shows an appreciable increase from one survey-year to another, represented by the vertical distances between the lines on Figure 6.4. This reflects the reduction in 'real' labour requirements which took place.

For our present purpose, however, we are more concerned with the differences in labour performances between size-groups than with differences between years. Figure 6.4 shows that this measure of output per unit of labour consistently indicated, irrespective of year, a rapid rate of increase with size of farm up to about 10 ha. (25 acres) with a somewhat slower rate of increase thereafter, but with no suggestion that performance tended to stabilise once a certain size of farm had been reached. If there is indeed such a 'ceiling' in this respect, the results for 1963 suggest that it was tending to move further up the size scale. It must be noted, however, that these surveys were confined to small farms; and although some of them were of over 30 ha. (74 acres) these were relatively few and cannot be accurately represented in Figure 6.4. Since we do not know their size distribution, but only that the average size in the top group was 42·6 ha. (106 acres) in 1957, we must look elsewhere for evidence that, in the Netherlands, as in Britain, there are limits to the range of size over which economies of size in the use of labour appear to prevail.

Before doing so, however, the extent of the apparent diseconomy of labour on the smallest of these Dutch farms may be noted. In order to facilitate direct comparison between size-groups, irrespective of year, the figures of Table 6.12 have been converted in Table 6.13 into index numbers of output per unit of labour input based on the data for the 10–12 ha. size-group in each year.

The final column of this table summarises the relationship, and shows that – according to this particular measure – average output per unit of labour on sandy-soil farms of 10–12 ha. was almost twice as much as on farms of 1–3 ha., while moving up the scale to 20–30 ha. added only a further 21 per cent to labour performance.

A further survey of farms of the same regions in 1968 showed similar labour performance relationships between size-groups, but as the basis of measurement was different, the figures are not included in Table 6.13. It was noticeable, however, that the relative diseconomy of the smallest farms had been considerably reduced, and this is attributable to the rapid disappearance of many of the uneconomic farms in these groups and the development of specialised pig or poultry farming on some of those which remained, compensating for their lack of land.[29]

Table 6.13
Index of output per unit of labour input on different
sizes of small farms in the Netherlands sandy soil regions

Size-groups (hectares)	Average number of hectares	Index of output per unit of labour input, in standard hours per labour unit (10–12 ha. group = 100)				
	(1957)	1948	1952	1957	1963	Average 1948–63
1–3	2·2	48	56	58	55	54
3–5	4·1	69	70	71	64	69
5–7	5·9	81	79	86	69	79
7–10	8·4	95	91	95	83	91
10–12	10·9	100	100	100	100	100
12–15	13·3	103	103	108	101	104
15–20	17·0	114	109	120	108	112
20–30	23·8	126	116	131	113	121
30 and over	42·6	132	140	145	159	141

Since 1968, a different measure of labour performance has been used in the Netherlands, namely 'SBE per full-time worker'. SBE stands for 'standaard-bedrijfseenheden'. It is a coefficient, or standard unit, which varies between the different kinds of crops and livestock according to their 'net value added'. It represents the factor costs of the various activities on a modern farm of a size sufficient to provide full-time work in 1968, at price levels of that year, when one SBE was equivalent to 200 guilders factor cost (labour and management, interest on invested capital and net rent). The total SBE of a farm is used as a criterion for size-classification, and the percentage distribution of SBE between the various enterprises on the farm is used as a basis for type-classification — for example, into arable, livestock (cattle), pig and poultry farms, etc. In 1968, a size of 90 SBE was regarded for purposes of price policy as a 'threshold' size, and this 'threshold' is raised by about 3–5 per cent a year to allow for increasing productivity. Table 6.14 shows the relationship between size of farm as measured in SBE and labour performance as measured in SBE per regular male worker calculated from a sample drawn from the 1968 census returns.

Although SBE is a measure of size of business and not of the farm area, the Dutch figures show the familiar positive relationship between size and labour performance.

Table 6.14
Labour performance and size of farm in the
Netherlands, 1968

SBE size group	< 30	30–50	50–70	70–90	90–110	110–150	150–190	> 190	Average, all sizes
Regular male workers per farm	1·06	1·20	1·25	1·33	1·42	1·64	2·00	2·85	1·42
SBE per regular male worker	17	34	47	60	69	77	84	93	59
Share in total number of SBE (per cent)	3	7	12	16	15	21	11	15	100

Note: The table relates to agricultural holdings (excluding horticultural holdings) whose operators had farming as their main occupation.

Source: de Veer, J. *Bedrijfsomvang en arbeidsproductiviteit. Mededelingen en overdrukken 55,* Landbouw-Economisch Instituut, The Hague, 1971.

The farm accounts collected in the Netherlands by the Landbouw-Economisch Instituut have been analysed to show the relationship between size and labour performance discussed above. The results for 1968/69 and for 1971/72, for various types of farm, are shown in Figures 6.5 and 6.6 The resemblance to other results, already given, will be readily apparent. In 1968/69 labour performance increased most sharply up to about 100–110 SBE while, in 1971/72, the corresponding point appeared to be at about 125 SBE. The number of man units actually working (not theoretically required) on the farms at these points was about 1·5, both in 1968/69 and in 1971/72.

From the same source of farm accounting data, we have derived output/total input ratios of the kind already discussed for England and Wales — that is, total value of output per 100 guilders of total costs, including imputed costs of the labour of the farmer and his family (Figure 6.7). The consistency of the respective efficiency ratios between the two years, and their similarity to the figures for England and Wales, are striking features of these data. The extent to which the imputed cost of the labour of the farmer and his family dominates the cost structure on the smaller farms can be seen from Figure 6.8. Both on arable and dairy farms, the percentage of this cost in relation to total costs was tending to increase between 1968/69 and 1971/72 throughout the range of farm sizes.

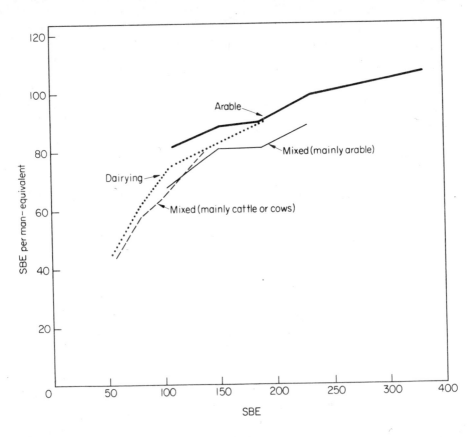

Fig. 6.5 Size of farm business and labour performance by type of farming, Netherlands, 1968/69

This Dutch work, the Irish and the two UK sources (FMS and the Economic Development Committee for Agriculture), which were all whole business as opposed to single enterprise studies, clearly show the widespread importance of the labour of the farmer and his immediate family in contributing to economies of size through the greater spread of their labour's value. Because this family labour forms a surplus principally on the smallest farms and diminishes rapidly as larger sizes are encountered, it is perhaps more appropriate to describe the labour penalty as a diseconomy suffered by small farms because of its indivisible nature, rather than as an economy of large size.

144

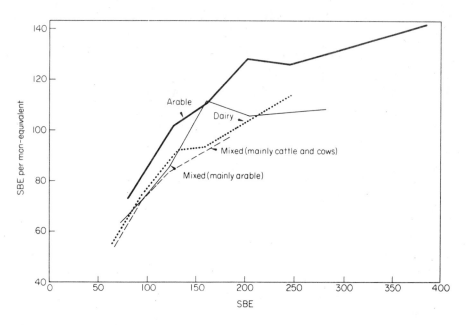

Fig. 6.6   Size of farm business and labour performance by type of farming, Netherlands, 1971/72

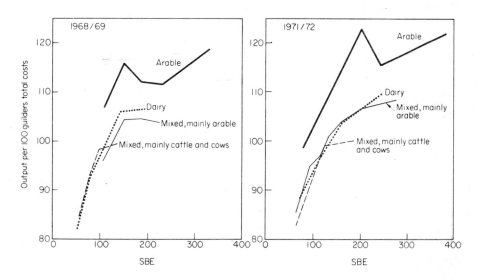

Fig. 6.7   Size of farm business and efficiency ratio by type of farming, Netherlands, 1968/69 and 1971/72

145

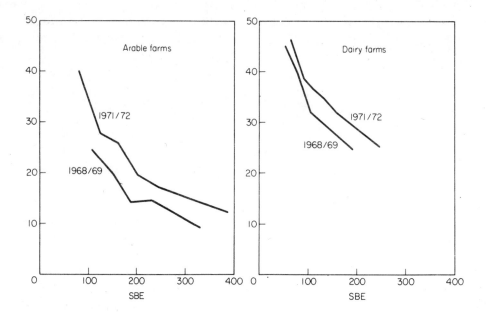

Fig. 6.8 Imputed cost of labour of farmer and family as percentage of total costs, by size of business, Netherlands, 1968/69 and 1971/72

Some other studies in the UK and abroad

A British study (by Scott) which made its approach to identifying economies of size through model building, [30] concluded that the indivisibility and immobility of labour was primarily responsible for the diseconomies of small farms; only on cropping farms was the indivisibility of machinery a severe constraint.

Studies in Australia and the USA suggest that the general pattern of economies of size is widespread — significant economies are gained by medium-sized farms over small farms but large farms do not appear to gain further economies. However, in those countries the economies of size stemming from mechanisation are more widespread than in the UK.

A recent study in Australia found that two general groups of farm types could be identified. In the first, which included sheep, wheat and dairy farms, [31] the evidence suggested that significant economies of size existed for small to medium-size farms, and thereafter average costs remained roughly constant. In the second group, which included beef production and most of the fruit-growing industry, there was no clear evidence of economies of size. It is interesting to note that in Australia (and also in the USA), the normal yardstick of size is the value of the farm's output, not acreage or standard man-days, as in the UK. The economies achieved in Australia were attributed to the greater spreading of lumpy overheads, and on wheat farms this means that lowest costs were incurred when the large machinery was used at full capacity, with no further economies of size to be gained. In the Australian context, less importance appears to be placed on the labour of the farmer himself as a potential source of economies, but this is probably due to the larger-scale structure of Australian farming.

In the USA, a similar situation is found. For example, on dairy farms in Minnesota [32] substantial economies were found as the level of output was increased up to the largest two-man dairy farm, but the further decline in costs achieved by three- and four-man farms was at a much slower rate. The importance of utilising 'discrete' resources is again given as the origin of economies of size in a study of the Blackland area of Texas [33] where average costs per unit of production were found to decrease rapidly as output neared full employment of the regular labour force and full utilisation of the field equipment. Madden has summarised research in the area of economies of size [34] and has shown that, when a crop farm reaches a one-man to two-man level of operation, it has realised all the cost economies of size. Fundamentally, the Australian and USA evidence is in line with that from the UK in that *almost all studies suggest that the long-run average cost curve for farming is not U-shaped, which would suggest economies of size up to a certain size of operation followed by diseconomies, but that it is L-shaped, implying economies of size up to a certain size followed by neither diseconomies nor economies as larger-sized production units are encountered.*

Appendix: evidence relating to single enterprises

Studies of individual enterprises are a supplementary source of information on economies of farm size. They must be treated as secondary to studies embracing the whole farm business because enterprise studies usually involve the allocation of costs of 'discrete' resources — for example, the depreciation of a combine on a cropping farm may have to be allocated between wheat, barley, oats and beans if each enterprise is to be costed separately. The basis of allocation — acreage, weight of crop, value, or time spent — is somewhat arbitrary and yet can have a critical effect on the existence of economies of size. It was to obviate such problems that gross-margin analysis has been developed to replace full-cost accounting as an aid to farm management decisions.

A related characteristic of single-enterprise studies on multi-enterprise farms is that, because the economies of size shown to exist for one enterprise may be partially or completely offset, or even more than offset, by diseconomies in other enterprises, the whole business may not reflect the economies of size experienced with just one of its component parts. Naturally, these objections are of reduced importance where the overwhelming proportion of a farm's production is concerned with one enterprise, as might be the case on a specialist dairy farm or a cereal farm. Enterprise studies, then, must be treated with caution as they are only partial measures of a business, although they can also yield valuable information on potential sources of economies of size, from which the whole business may (or may not) be able to benefit.

Two of the land-demanding enterprises — milk production and cereal production [35] — have received more attention than others from economists with regard to economies of size, although the identification of economies of size has usually been the by-product of research into other aspects of the enterprises. The by no means conclusive evidence for economies of size in these two important enterprises is summarised below.

Prima facie case for enterprise economies of size

Just as the decline over the years in the number of small farm businesses and the growth in numbers of large ones can be taken to infer the existence of economies of size, so the change in the size structure of single enterprises present a *prima facie* case for economies, although such changes *could* be caused by factors not directly or wholly attributable to the enterprise in question.

148

Table 6.15 shows that a feature of all major enterprises in England and Wales over the 1960s was a concentration of production into fewer but larger units. With the exception of beef cows and barley, this has continued in the early 1970s. Three indicators of this trend are: the falling number of producers; the rising average size of enterprise; and the rising proportion of the land area or of the livestock population found in the larger units. Of particular relevance here is the average size of enterprise, and figures for each all tell the same story of rising averages – and a similar picture could be shown for Scotland and Northern Ireland. For example, the average area of cereals per grower more than doubled during the period 1960–73, and dairy and beef herds expanded at a similar rate. The most dramatic increase was in the average number of broilers per producer, from 2,000 in 1960 to 24,000 in 1973.

Some of these trends appear to be still gathering momentum; the annual changes in average size of dairy, breeding ewe and breeding pig enterprises since 1970 have been more rapid than those which took place between 1965 and 1970. The Milk Marketing Board has suggested that, by 1980, the average size of dairy herd in the UK may be 50 cows (compared with 39 in 1973). However, the changes in relative costs and prices experienced since the United Kingdom joined the EEC have reversed the decline in the number of beef-cow herds (though not the average size of enterprise) and halted the rise in the average barley acreage.

The milk enterprise

Milk production has been the most important single enterprise in the UK for several decades, currently accounting for about a fifth of total agricultural output. A look at evidence on costs of production with herds of different sizes is preferable to inferences about economies of size from changing herd sizes, and this is made possible by the attention which this important enterprise has received through the MAFF's and the Milk Marketing Board's studies of the costs of production.

It appears overall that economies of size are experienced up to the 60 cow herd; from 60 to 200 cows, little or no further economies are available; herds larger than 200 cows again experience economies, but such herds are not numerous, and the particular circumstances which make them technically viable, including the ability to divide the herd into smaller operational units, probably occur too infrequently to enable them to be used as a goal to which smaller herds should expand.

Cost compositions are closely allied with the techniques of production

149

Table 6.15

Concentration of enterprises on agricultural holdings, England and Wales, 1960, 1965, 1970 and 1973

	Number of producers ('000)				Average size of enterprise				Percentage in large units			
	1960	1965	1970	1973	1960	1965	1970	1973	1960	1965	1970	1973
Dairy cows	140	114	85	74	19	23	32	39	100 cows and over			
									3·9	6·9	14·8	21·6
Beef cows	64	61	55	57	8	9	12	15	100 cows and over			
									3·7	5·2	9·1	10·7
Breeding ewes	88	84	62	58	100	114	136	159	500 ewes and over			
									15·0	20·9	26·9	31·7
Breeding pigs	82	73	45	35	7	9	17	24	100 sows and over			
									6·8	11·0	24·0	35·7
Laying fowls	216	158	85*	70	158	257	478*	572	5,000 birds and over			
									4·3	21·0	65·1*	72·8
Broilers †	6	3	2	2	2	9	22	24	50,000 birds and over			
									16·6	48·0	67·2	72·2
Wheat	78	65	45	44	26	37	53	63	100 acres and over			
									26·1	41·7	53·5	60·8
Barley	91	106	80	77	34	44	60	60	100 acres and over			
									40·6	50·3	59·3	59·0
All cereals	147	131	96	90	43	58	82	89	200 acres and over			
									27·3	39·4	50·3	53·2
Potatoes (main crop)	92	66	47	38	5	7	9	10	100 acres and over			
									5·4	10·8	13·2	12·7

* 1971
† Average size of enterprise is in units of 1000 birds.
Source: Derived from MAFF *Agricultural Statistics* (various years).

used, and these are, in turn, closely associated with herd size. For example, a recent survey found that 61 per cent of all herds between 41 and 60 cows were milked in cowsheds, but this proportion fell to 4 per cent for herds of 101–120 cows. [36] Cowshed milking inevitably involves a greater expenditure on labour per cow, and this is reflected in the apparent economy of size which occurs when moving from the small to medium-sized herds. Figure 6.9 gives a generalised picture of the relationship between herd size and labour use per cow for 1968/69, and incorporates the different methods of milking used. The cowshed method of milking is not common in herds of 60 cows and more (13 per cent or less of installations) so that the line in Figure 6.9 representing labour used in cowsheds can be discounted beyond that size. The overall impression is then gained that, while labour used per cow falls up to the 70 or 80 cow level, little or no further economies are gained from this source.

Economy in the use of labour raises the question whether this result entails an excessive use of capital, but a categorical answer cannot be given. On one hand, there is evidence that economies of size in the use of buildings occur; the building floor-space utilised per cow by herds of 40–59 cows is much less than with herds of 20–39 cows (5·2 m² as opposed to 9·6 m²), and this must again be closely linked with the type of housing. [37] With more than 60 cows little further space is saved. On the other hand, a survey in 1968/69 [38] found that farms with herds of 40 cows and above invested approximately twice as much capital in dairy equipment per cow as did farms with under 40 cows. This was explained by the sparseness of equipment in small herds coupled with the tendency of large herds to maintain a modern stock of equipment to secure all the economies possible in the use of labour. In addition, there was a tendency for cow values to rise with increasing size of herd, which might have been indicative of better quality stock.

The most recent information on the costs of milk production, [39] relating to 1972/73, gives the cost of producing a gallon of milk, the returns per gallon, and the margin between returns and costs in herds of different sizes (see Table 6.16). This form of presentation thus takes into account both differences in costs and in yields per cow. Because returns (or value of output) per cow do not vary greatly between herd sizes, cow numbers can be used as a reasonable proxy for output as a measure of enterprise size. (It should be recalled that output is the conventional criterion of size when economies of size are discussed.)

Feed is the single most important item in the cost structure of milk production, contributing over half of the total costs involved. Table 6.16 shows that the feed costs per gallon in herds declined by small (but

151

Table 6.16
Average costs, returns and margins of milk production by

Item	6·0–9·9	10·0–19·9	20·0–29·9
Number of herds: in sample	12	62	89
in raised sample	4,889	14,497	13,171
Herd size (cows)	3·6	15·1	24·8
Farm size (acres)	41	69	83
Labour (hours per cow)	139	112	87
Seasonality (winter gallons as percentage of year)	42·3	42·1	43·9
Yield (gallons per cow)	738	803	842
Dry cows (percentage of total cows)	20·4	18·8	18·5
Stocking rate (forage acres per cow)	2·16	1·76	1·62
Units of nitrogen (per acre)	31	50	58
Purchased concentrates (cwt per cow)	19·9	20·2	23·3
Home-grown concentrates (cwt per cow)	2·3	4·4	3·2
Total concentrates (cwt per cow)	22·2	24·6	26·5
Total concentrates (lb per gallon)	3·4	3·4	3·5
Hay and straw (cwt per cow)	35·0	31·5	31·4
Silage (cwt per cow)	6·3	6·3	7·6
Kale (cwt per cow)	9·7	7·0	6·5
Roots, green fodder and other (cwt per cow)	7·6	9·3	7·8
Feeds: Purchased (p)	6·28	5·79	6·06
Home-grown (p)	2·50	2·47	2·03
Grazing (p)	2·13	1·71	1·48
Total	10·91	9·97	9·57
Labour: Paid (p)	1·11	0·75	0·64
Unpaid (p): farmer and wife	8·10	6·01	3·92
other	1·10	1·01	1·16
total	9·20	7·02	5·08
Total	10·31	7·77	5·72
Miscellaneous (p)	5·13	4·66	4·10
Herd replacement (p)	1·18	0·52	0·60
Gross farm costs (p)	27·53	22·92	19·99
Milk returns (p)	19·64	20·73	20·25
Value of calves (p)	4·54	3·99	4·06
Gross returns (p)	24·18	24·72	24·31
Management and investment income (p)	−3·35	1·80	4·32
Set farm income (p)	4·75	7·81	8·24
Family income (p)	5·85	8·82	9·40

Source: Milk Marketing Board, *Costs of Milk Production in England and*

herd size-group, 1972/73 (pence per gallon)

Herd size (cows)						200.0 and over	Total
30.0–39.9	40.0–49.9	50.0–59.9	60.0–69.9	70.0–99.9	100.0–199.9		
67	54	45	39	63	30	9	470
10,226	7,421	5,215	3,913	5,781	3,071	474	68,658
34.7	44.6	54.0	64.9	82.2	131.5	323.3	41.4
98	116	183	212	234	439	1,103	134
70	58	51	46	41	40	34	60
47.0	47.9	47.9	46.0	49.9	51.2	52.2	45.5
885	884	913	907	955	1,003	905	906
18.2	15.8	17.7	16.9	16.6	16.9	15.1	17.3
1.41	1.36	1.39	1.52	1.34	1.22	1.17	1.42
104	108	141	130	179	198	234	95
23.3	24.0	22.9	19.2	24.9	24.2	21.3	23.0
3.7	3.4	5.3	4.2	4.3	7.2	5.6	4.5
27.0	27.4	28.2	23.4	29.2	31.4	26.9	27.5
3.4	3.5	3.5	2.9	3.4	3.5	3.3	3.4
24.9	25.8	22.4	25.0	16.0	11.1	9.2	21.9
21.1	26.0	39.3	34.5	61.1	66.8	79.1	38.1
7.4	6.2	12.8	11.5	10.1	17.7	12.8	10.3
5.3	6.3	8.8	4.3	9.6	11.0	21.9	8.7
5.87	5.89	5.09	4.50	5.22	4.74	3.99	5.30
1.88	1.85	2.17	2.12	1.97	2.57	2.36	2.14
1.62	1.51	1.69	1.63	1.69	1.64	1.75	1.63
9.37	9.25	8.95	8.25	8.88	8.95	8.10	9.07
0.78	0.84	1.49	1.41	1.65	2.08	2.25	1.34
3.12	2.13	1.28	1.07	0.56	0.17	–	1.90
0.55	0.69	0.44	0.38	0.27	0.15	–	0.50
3.67	2.82	1.72	1.45	0.83	0.32	–	2.40
4.45	3.66	3.21	2.86	2.48	2.40	2.25	3.74
4.18	3.95	4.30	4.07	4.00	4.02	3.80	4.12
0.67	0.77	0.45	0.64	0.78	0.70	0.91	0.68
18.67	17.63	16.91	15.82	16.14	16.07	15.06	17.61
20.64	20.57	20.85	20.36	20.83	21.17	20.84	20.71
3.77	3.87	3.65	4.02	3.37	3.34	3.32	3.68
24.41	24.44	24.50	24.38	24.20	24.51	24.16	24.39
5.74	6.81	7.59	8.36	8.05	8.44	9.10	6.78
8.86	8.94	8.87	9.63	8.62	8.61	9.10	8.68
9.41	9.63	9.31	10.01	8.89	8.76	9.10	9.18

Wales, April 1972 to March 1973, 1974.

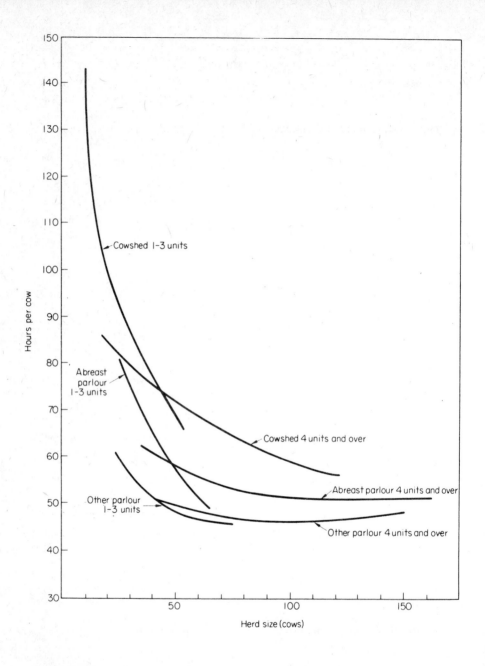

Fig. 6.9   Labour use according to herd size and system of milking

Source: MAFF *Costs and efficiency in milk production,* 1972.

154

statistically significant) steps up to the 60 cow herd, but, beyond that size, the cost per gallon remained at a stable level except for herds of 60–69·9 cows and herds above 200 cows, where feed costs were noticeably (and significantly) lower. Except for the two size-groups mentioned, feed does not appear to be a major source of economies of size.

Labour input, however, does form a major source. We have already established that economies in the use of labour occurred in 1968/69 up to the 70–80 cow herd, and this was again reflected in the costs of milk production for 1972/73. The labour cost per gallon fell steeply at first with increasing herd size (see Figure 6.10), but the greater part of the overall decline had been achieved at the 60 cow herd size. Nevertheless, the further labour economies of the larger herds were statistically

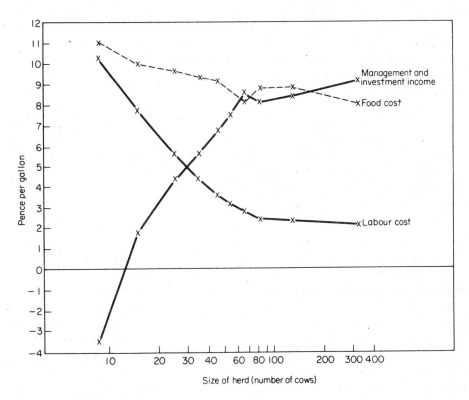

Fig. 6.10   Management and investment income and labour and food costs per gallon in dairy herds of different sizes, England and Wales, 1972/73

Source: derived from Milk Marketing Board *Costs of Milk Production in England and Wales April 1972 to March 1973*, 1974.

155

significant. The labour economies were the result of two components moving in contrary motion — the paid labour element increased beyond the 20 cow herd while the unpaid element, chiefly consisting of the farmer's and his wife's labour, fell dramatically. The decline in unpaid labour more than offset the rise in paid labour per gallon.

In terms of pence per gallon, the total gross cost of production (feed and labour accounting for about three-quarters of the total) fell with increasing herd size, although gains beyond the 50 cow herd were not great. In 1972/73 the 60—69 cow herds incurred noticeably lower costs per gallon, and were only bettered by herds of more than 200 cows.

But returns per gallon also varied a little with size of herd, attributable to both differences in milk quality and the value of calves, and this variation must also be taken into account when assessing economies of size. 'Gross returns minus gross farm costs' (including the value of the farmer's and wife's labour) is probably the best indicator of economies of size, with the size of the enterprise measured in numbers of cows. This margin is termed 'management and investment income per gallon', and it rose (although not continuously) over the range of herd sizes, indicating economies of size, with the largest economies occurring with movements away from the smallest herds (see Figure 6.10). The management and investment income per gallon of each size-group was significantly different (at the 5 per cent level of statistical significance or better) from that of the adjacent size-groups throughout the whole range of sizes.

An exception to the general gain of economies with size was provided by the 60—69·9 cow herds which performed significantly better than either the 50—69·9 cow herds or the 70—99·9 cow herds. Only the very largest herds (200 cows and over) possessed a significantly larger management and investment income per gallon. The superior performance of this group was also noted in surveys in 1965/66 and 1968/69.[38] Table 6.16 clearly shows that they managed to achieve their performance — which was not in itself unusually high in terms of output per cow or return per gallon — at a much lower feed cost, with a large saving in purchased feed (mainly concentrates), than herds in adjacent size-groups. We shall show later that these herds of 60—69·9 cows also used low stocking density on their forage acres, so at least part of their success appears to stem from a policy of substituting home-grown forage for purchased feedstuffs. However, as this was not reflected in higher costs of home-produced feed, we suspect that better management is important — perhaps this size of herd corresponded to the smallest at which a specialist cowman was justified and yet at which he still had sufficient time for feeding management of individual animals.

156

The 1972/73 data enable the very large herds (200 cows and over) to be compared with smaller ones, possibly for the first time. Hitherto, information on herds of over 100 cows has been too scanty to reliably identify economies of size, in spite of the fact that a large and growing percentage of the dairy cows in England and Wales is in herds of 100 cows or more — 21 per cent in 1973. The 1972/73 data show (Figure 6.10) that the management and investment income per gallon was highest in herds of 200 cows and over, and it was significantly greater than even the 60–69·9 cow herds. These largest herds used significantly less food, significantly less miscellaneous inputs, [40] and significantly less labour per gallon than herds of 100–199·9 cows, but not significantly less food than herds of 60–69·9 cows (although they used significantly less labour and miscellaneous inputs). Unfortunately, we do not know whether these very large herds are operated as single entities or whether they are subdivided into a number of smaller operational units. Herds of 100–199·9 cows were not significantly better performers in terms of management and investment income per gallon than the 60–69·9 cow herds, although they were better than the 70–99·9 cow herds. Taking an overall perspective, it appears that, although economies of size *do* occur, most of the gains are achieved by the time the herd of 60–69·9 cows is reached, and any subsequent gains are only produced by the very largest herds.

Intensity of land use

Land rents have already been built into the calculation of costs quoted above, but it is interesting to note that the larger herds generally used land more intensively than smaller ones. The management and investment income per forage acre rose throughout the herd-size spectrum, although, beyond 100 cows, the gain was negligible. On the other hand, the number of forage acres per cow dropped noticeably in herds of over 100 cows. A point to note is that the stocking density of herds of 60–69·9 cows was lower than that in adjacent size-groups, and less nitrogen fertilizer per acre was used, suggesting that their lower use of purchased concentrates was achieved by a more extensive use of land.

Profitability

A brief excursion into profitability, or return on capital, and dairy herd size, as opposed to efficiency of resource use, is of interest here. Management and investment income per herd can be expressed as a percentage of the capital which the operator has invested in the herd (see Table 6.17). For 1972/73, this percentage rose with increasing herd size, with the

60—69·9 herds again being rather higher than their position in the spectrum of herd sizes might lead one to expect, and the highest figure being achieved by the 200 and over cow herd size. Because of the discontinuity caused by the 60—69·9 cow herds, the gain in the percentage figure beyond this size-group was relatively small — the further gain to the 200 and over cow herds was less than the gain from the 50—59·9 cow herds to the 60—69·9 cow herds.

Table 6.17
Return on operator's capital by size of dairy-cow herd

Herd size (cows)	(a) Total operator's capital per herd[1] (£)	(b) Management and investment income per herd (£)	(b) as percentage of (a)
6·0— 9·9	1,492	−212	−14·2
10·0— 19·9	2,571	218	8·5
20·0— 29·9	4,636	904	19·5
30·0— 39·9	6,735	1,762	26·2
40·0— 49·9	8,877	2,681	30·2
50·0— 59·9	11,151	3,746	33·6
60·0— 69·9	13,111	5,036	38·4
70·0— 99·0	16,993	6,325	37·2
100·0—199·9	27,015	11,124	41·2
200 and over	62,161	26,603	42·8
All sizes	8,164	2,542	31·1

[1] Land is treated as rented. Operator's capital is valued at historical cost.
Source: Derived from *Costs of Milk Production in England and Wales, April 1972 to March 1973,* Milk Marketing Board, 1974.

These percentages cannot be regarded as a final net return on capital, as no allowance has been made for managerial input. It is quite likely that the largest herds require more managerial effort than those of 60—69·9 cows, and it is possible that this increment could nullify the fall in other costs to produce a less steeply rising, constant, or falling net return on capital beyond herds of 60 cows, depending on the price put on the incremental managerial effort. But this increment is not easily priced as it involves both an evaluation of total managerial effort, which would probably be based on some assessment of transfer earnings, and also the allocation of this effort between enterprises, a process infinitely more difficult than measuring the time the farmer spends in physical labour with his dairy herd, if only because it could be argued that a farmer could be thinking about his herd while physically involved with other enterprises.

The survey data quoted above relate to a cross-section of milk production on different farms and it cannot be assumed that, if a 50—59·9 cow herd were expanded to 100 cows, this would acquire the cost structure exhibited by existing 100 cow herds. In particular, one could argue that, for the very largest herds to be even technically viable, such special circumstances of soil type, land availability, access to capital, labour and management are required, and these circumstances occur so rarely, that a too emphatic statement that these herds are the most efficient might affect the industry's efficiency adversely by encouraging smaller enterprises to expand production to levels far beyond their managerial or physical capacity.[41]

Changes in economies of size with time

It must be remembered that the herd size by which most economies will have been reached is only the boundary for that particular set of price/ cost conditions and the techniques of production then in use. The 1950s and 1960s were marked by a decline in the number of labour hours used per cow, and this trend appears to be continuing. This occurred at all sizes of herds for which data are available (although this does not include herds above 100 cows) and must be largely explained by the falling out of use of labour-demanding cowshed milking systems. In Denmark, where a similar situation of labour reduction has occurred, it has been shown that, in addition, the size of herd at which labour requirements are minimal has tended to rise.[42] This is illustrated in Figure 6.11. It seems likely that a similar situation obtained in England and Wales, especially as the mean size of farm and the number of large herds continue to rise.

One important aspect of the reduction in labour requirements is that the small and medium-sized herds have become increasingly dependent on farmer and family labour. This is shown in Table 6.18. Whether this has come about through farmers dispensing with or failing to retain paid labour, or by herd expansion where the farmer and family already comprised the whole force cannot be immediately detected, but it is evident that a greater spreading of the 'discrete' or 'indivisible' resource of the farmer's labour over a greater volume of production has been going on. In doing so, they have been on the path by which larger businesses

159

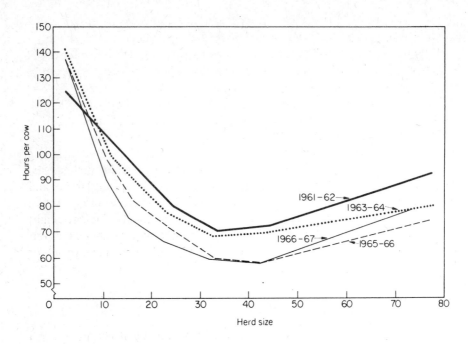

Fig. 6.11   Hours per cow by herd size, Denmark

Source: Silvey, D.R., *Milk Production: a comparison of England and Denmark*, Agricultural Economics Unit, Department of Land Economy, University of Cambridge, 1973.

Table 6.18
Distribution of herds by type of labour within
herd size-groups, 1965/66 and 1968/69

| Herd size (cows) | Distribution of herds (per cent) | | | | | |
| | Family labour only | | Family and paid labour | | Paid labour only | |
	1965/66	1968/69	1965/66	1968/69	1965/66	1968/69
Under 10	82	91	18	9	—	—
10–19·9	75	91	20	7	5	2
20–29·9	44	70	52	29	4	1
30–39·9	31	58	59	40	10	2
40–49·9	21	29	57	64	22	7
50–69·9	5	13	64	67	31	20
70–99·9	3	11	47	61	50	28
100 and over	—	—	24	30	76	72
All herds	51	62	39	31	10	7

Source: MAFF *Costs and efficiency in milk production 1968–1969*, 1972.

achieve economies of size and greater efficiency. Perhaps this is why the performance in terms of output per £100 input of small specialist dairy businesses (that is, farms where the dairy enterprise is dominant) appears to be more in line with that of larger dairy businesses, more so than with other types of farming (see Figure 6.4).

Cereal enterprises

Cereals account for about one eighth of the total value of agricultural output in the UK and occupy over half the arable acreage, or just under a third of the total area of crops and grass. The production of cereals has been described as probably the most straightforward type of farm work,[43] requiring a relatively low input of labour and capital per acre, despite the probable high degree of mechanisation. Because economies of size in the use of field machinery and storage equipment can theoretically be easily demonstrated, they might be expected to exist in practice.

However, if there are economies of size, they do not arise from the use of the combined variable inputs of production (fertilizer plus seeds plus sprays). Reference to the gross margin tables in recent issues of the annual *Farm Incomes in England and Wales* reports of MAFF shows that the value of output per acre for wheat, barley and oats is closely similar in each of the four categories of size (0–49·9, 50–99·9, 100–299·9, 300+ acres), except possibly for the 0–49·9 acre category of wheat production, where output is a little lower. (The lack of standard errors prevents statistically significant differences from being established.) However, these smallest growers tend to use lower quantities of variable inputs so that their gross margin per £100 output (value of output minus variable costs) is not noticeably worse than that of larger growers; indeed, in 1972/73 it tended to be greater (except for spring oats). No economies of size are thus evident from variable inputs in the cereal enterprises. The MAFF publication does not attempt to allocate fixed costs to cereal production, and we must turn to other enterprise studies for this information, which is more likely to give evidence of economies of size.

The report of the National Wheat Survey[44] relating to the 1964 crop provides valuable, although now rather dated, information on the economies of size experienced with this cereal. Information on costs of production was gathered from 282 farms. The size of enterprise was measured in acres. As yields per acre did not vary significantly between size-groups, acreage size-groups could be taken to imply output (volume) size-groups. Production costs were expressed per ton of wheat, but, for

Table 6.19

Effect of size of wheat acreage

Wheat acreage size-group	¼–9¾	10–29¾	30–69¾	70–299¾	300+	Total
Variable costs (£ per ton)	6·3	5·6	5·0	4·6	4·2	4·9
s.e.	(0·54)	(0·21)	(0·19)	(0·12)	(0·34)	(0·092)
Fixed costs excluding rent (£ per ton)	6·9	7·1	7·8	7·5	7·3	7·5
s.e.	(0·37)	(0·25)	(0·25)	(0·16)	(0·47)	(0·11)
Total costs excluding rent (£ per ton)	13·6	12·3	13·2	12·4	11·8	12·6
s.e	(0·51)	(0·28)	(0·31)	(0·19)	(0·44)	(0·11)
Grain sales (£ per ton)	24·1	24·9	26·1	26·5	27·6	26·0
s.e.	(1·30)	(0·62)	(0·68)	(0·50)	(1·45)	(0·33)
Gross margin (£ per ton)	17·8	19·8	21·1	21·8	23·5	21·0
s.e	(1·76)	(0·67)	(0·72)	0·52	(1·55)	(0·35)
Net margin excluding rent (£ per ton)	10·8	12·6	13·2	14·4	16·1	13·6
s.e.	(2·0)	(0·78)	(0·84)	(0·63)	(1·60)	(0·42)
Margin over materials (£ per ton)	20·0	21·4	22·2	22·5	23·6	22·1
s.e.	(1·70)	(0·64)	(0·68)	(0·52)	(1·56)	(0·34)
Regular labour cost (£ per ton)	1·88	1·65	1·43	1·14	1·01	1·35
s.e.	(0·274)	(0·086)	(0·076)	(0·045)	(0·08)	(0·034)
Machinery cost including tractors (£ per ton)	2·60	2·63	3·31	3·18	3·09	3·05
s.e.	(0·37)	(0·15)	(0·16)	(0·09)	(0·15)	(0·07)

Table 6.19 continued

Wheat acreage size-group	¼–9¾	10–29¾	30–69¾	70–299¾	300+	Total
Combine harvester costs (£ per ton)	1·12	1·28	1·45	1·42	1·42	1·39
s.e.	(0·13)	(0·10)	(0·09)	(0·04)	(0·09)	(0·07)
Labour use:						
Overall labour-hours per ton (including straw disposal)	9·0	7·6	6·3	4·6	4·4	6·0
Combine harvesting* (labour-hours per ton)	1·82	1·61	1·25	1·01	0·76	1·23
Yield (tons per acre)	1·68	1·75	1·71	1·78	1·76	1·75
s.e.	(0·097)	(0·039)	(0·043)	(0·029)	(0·104)	(0·02)
Seasonality index of sales	1·60	2·39	2·90	3·34	3·77	2·84

s.e. = standard error
*Means for farms reporting.

Source: Jackson, B.G., and Sturrock, F.G. *The National Wheat Survey: a report on a survey of the 1964 wheat crop in England and Wales*, Agricultural Economics Unit, Department of Land Economy, University of Cambridge, 1969 (p. 33).

the same reason, in most cases it would have been possible to use figures expressed per acre to show economies of size. The results from the survey are shown in Table 6.19. While sales and variable costs were taken from actual data, some of the fixed costs (for example the drier and storage depreciation charges), were based on standardised charges. The labour charge was calculated by applying standard wage rates to the actual number of hours worked and hence did not reflect inter-farm variations in wage rates. Rent charges were excluded partly because it was felt that they were affected by items such as livestock buildings which were irrelevant to wheat production, and partly because they were merely estimates on owner-occupied holdings. A valuable aspect of this study was that the calculation of standard errors permitted differences between means to be tested for statistical significance.

As has already been indicated, the size of the enterprise (cereal acreage) was not significant in explaining variations in yields, and this also applied to gross margins per acre (sales less variable costs). However, larger growers achieved significantly higher sales of grain in terms of average price received per ton. This was not because of a better bargaining position endowed purely by size, but because they were more able to store their grain until times when prices rose.

Mean gross margins increased consistently over the five acreage groups, but a considerable part of this was caused by differences in the use of contract services. Smaller growers tended to make greater use of contractors, thereby increasing costs and reducing gross margins. If contract charges were excluded, the resulting margin ('margin over materials') again showed a consistent rise with size of wheat enterprise, but this rise was not statistically significant. No economies of size were thus evident from the use of variable inputs.

Total production costs per ton (variable plus fixed costs) decreased with size and much of this difference was attributable to the contract costs already mentioned. Thus, fixed costs (mainly labour plus machinery costs) remained very constant, suggesting that, all other things being equal, smaller growers needed contract services even though their fixed costs per ton were similar to larger growers. Thus no economies of size stemmed in practice from the inputs which, combined, constituted fixed costs.

However, individual items of fixed costs did exhibit significant economies of size. Regular labour costs per ton decreased as size increased, and the input in labour hours per ton in the largest size-group was less than half that in the smallest. Part of this difference, however, was attributable to the fact that a higher proportion of large growers burned their straw. The average number of hours spent combining

164

declined very markedly as acreage increased, but the combine harvester costs in each size-group indicated that the increase in labour efficiency involved some extra machinery costs. Indeed, this appeared true of the whole labour/machinery complex, so that no significant economies in total fixed costs were achieved. The machinery figures should be treated with caution, however, as standard values were incorporated in this item, but it must be generally concluded that the size of wheat enterprise did not significantly influence the overall unit cost (variable plus fixed) of production. In other words, the 1964 National Wheat Survey did not reveal any significant economies of size.

Somewhat conflicting evidence on economies of size achieved with fixed costs is provided by a study of oat production in Scotland. [45] Here, the combined costs of labour, machinery, equipment and buildings declined with increasing cereal acreage (see Table 6.20). To be comparable with fixed costs as measured by the National Wheat Survey, the cost of contract and casual work must be deducted, but this still results in a decline with increasing size. The lack of standard errors prevents statistical significance from being ascribed to this decline. Within the total 'fixed' costs, regular labour cost per acre declined, but the cost of machinery first increased and then fell. The extensive use of binders on small acreages must be noted — demanding of labour but low in machinery cost and not requiring expensive buildings for grain storage — and the economies which the medium acreage growers gained over the small was through the substitution of capital for labour. However, the trend of lower costs with increasing cereal acreage was maintained amongst the farms with 50 acres of cereals or more, where the use of the binder was negligible. The larger growers still achieved some economies in the use of labour and tractors, perhaps through the use of larger implements and machines, and their investment in machinery was also lower per cereal acre because of the larger acreages handled.

Supporting evidence for the existence of economics of size attributable to 'fixed' inputs also comes from Scotland in the form of data collected on the costs of barley growing in the north of Scotland [46] (see Table 6.21). The conclusion drawn was that costs were considerably higher when less than 75 acres of cereals were grown, but that there was no indication of further economies beyond that size. This occurred even if contract (and casual labour) charges were excluded. The fall in costs was caused by a decline in tractor and general labour costs; however, any economies must be viewed with caution as these are the result of a somewhat arbitrary process of allocation. The per acre costs of *specialist* machinery, equipment and buildings (where the problem of allocation was much more simple) tended to be lower on the smaller enterprises. [47]

Table 6.20
Economics of oat production in Scotland: labour, machinery,
equipment and building costs in relation to acreage of cereals grown

Cereal acreage	Under 20 acres	20—49 acres	50—99 acres	100—199 acres	200 acres and over
Number of farms	37	47	29	16	12
Number of farmers using binder	20	15	2	1	—
Initial capital investment (£ per acre)					
Portable and field machinery	9·2	16·1	21·9	19·2	14·6
Durable equipment and buildings	2·4	2·5	13·7	13·3	16·0
Total	11·6	18·6	35·6	32·5	30·6
Estimated depreciation and repair costs (£ per acre)					
Portable and field machinery	1·9	3·2	4·4	3·8	2·9
Durable equipment and buildings	0·2	0·3	1·4	1·3	1·6
Total (A)	2·1	3·5	5·8	5·1	4·5
Cost of contract and casual work (B)	3·5	3·6	2·1	1·0	0·7
Regular labour (man hours per acre)	17·6	12·7	10·0	7·2	6·9
Estimated cost (C), (£ per acre)	8·4	6·1	4·8	3·5	3·3
Tractor work (tractor hours per acre)	9·1	7·9	7·2	6·2	5·8
Estimated cost (D), (£ per acre)	2·7	2·4	2·1	1·9	1·7
Total machinery, buildings and labour costs (A + B + C + D)	16·7	15·6	14·8	11·5	10·2
Total costs, less contract and casual work (A + C + D)	13·2	12·0	12·7	10·5	9·5

Source: *The Economics of Oat Production in Scotland,* North of Scotland College of Agriculture, Agricultural Economics Division, School of Agriculture, Aberdeen.

Table 6.21
Labour and machinery costs in relation to cereal acreage

Cereal acreage group	Small	Medium	Large	Very large
Range of cereal acreage	27–76	77–132	133–220	221–590
Number of growers	13	15	13	13
Average cereal acreage	44	107	176	316
Contract work and casual labour (£ per acre)	2·7	1·2	0·8	0·8
Depreciation and repairs for specialised machinery, equipment and buildings (£ per acre)	3·9	4·1	4·3	4·2
Regular labour (£ per acre)	3·5	2·1	2·2	2·4
Tractor work (£ per acre)	1·5	1·1	1·2	1·2
Total of above (£ per acre)	11·6	8·5	8·5	8·6
Net margin (£ per acre)	7·4	11·3	13·7	11·3

Source: Sutherland, R.M., and Steele, R.J.G. *The Economics of Barley Production in the North of Scotland 1968,* North of Scotland College of Agriculture Economic Report 127, 1970.

It seems unlikely that the English (wheat) and Scottish (oats and barley) situations are sufficiently different for economies of size to be absent in the former country and present in the latter. We think that economies of size do generally occur in cereal growing, at least up to a certain size of enterprise. This is supported circumstantially by the rise in average size of cereals enterprise per farm. [48] Also, on the 'mainly cereal cropping farms' of the FMS in 1971/72, the combined labour and machinery costs (which are the principal components of fixed costs) per acre of crops and grass appeared noticeably higher in the smallest group of businesses (with an average acreage of 155 acres) than the next size-group (mean acreage 321 acres) or larger groups. [49]

A complication involved in drawing reliable inferences from data on fixed costs is that the 'standards' frequently employed can introduce distortion. For example, it has been suggested that growers with large enterprises tend to use newer machinery than smaller growers because of the greater attractiveness of tax concessions at high marginal rates of tax. The depreciation charge for large growers may thus tend to be greater.

The distorting effect of taxation hence could hide the manifestation of economies of size where they might be anticipated. Another complication, mentioned earlier, is that rates of depreciation are 'standards', and the actual rate of depreciation with a lightly used machine on a small enterprise may be less than that incorporated into farm accounts. Correcting for this would tend to erode any economies of size arising from machinery charges.

Studies of cereals production in Australia and the USA support the contention that economies of size exist, at least in their contexts. In an important wheat-growing area of New South Wales it was found [50] that the total cost of production (comprising variable and fixed costs, plus, in this instance, an allowance for interest on capital invested and wages of the operator) fell with increasing size but at a declining rate. Beyond a certain size (in the New South Wales context about 1,000 acres), no further economies were evident. A similar picture emerged even if operator wages and capital charges were excluded, although the initial decline in costs with increasing size was less sharp. An interesting feature of the results is that they support the idea of the 'module' — at about 1,000 acres one large set of cultivating and harvesting equipment was being used at maximum technical capacity, and increasing the acreage of the enterprise further resulted in a significant increase in costs. However, a gradual fall occurred with further acreage gains so that the costs for wheat-growers harvesting about 2,500 acres, the average costs (per bushel) were very much the same as for those harvesting 1,000 acres. These economies of size clearly arise from spreading machinery costs over larger outputs.

Similar evidence comes from the USA. In a study of wheat production costs and economies of enterprise size in the Nebraska Panhandle, [51] significant economies were experienced up to enterprises of 250 acres. From 250–300 acres, little size economies were realised, and above about 300 acres there appeared to be no further economies in the wheat enterprise, at least over the range of sizes studied. Variable costs of wheat production were nearly the same for all size classes; the economies of size resulted from the reduction in operator labour and machinery-related fixed costs as wheat enterprise size increased from the smallest size-group (less than 90 acres) to 300 acres.

When examined in the light of the evidence from Australia and the USA, cereal production in the UK would seem likely to exhibit a similar pattern of diminishing economies of size — not arising from variable inputs, but from 'discrete' inputs — eventually arriving at a point beyond which no further economies are noticeable. However it must be recalled that the allocation of fixed costs between enterprises is always somewhat arbitrary, and so such apparent economies, or in the case of the National Wheat Survey, the lack of economies, must be treated with caution. On balance, however, we are prepared to believe that such economies do exist for cereal growing in the UK.

Notes

[1] An American report has called attention to the fact that studies of large-scale farming have usually ignored the economies obtained from buying and selling in bulk. It noted that 'for almost all purchased inputs, discounts appeared to increase with size of farm unit'. Krause, K.R., and Kyle, L.R. *Midwestern Corn Farms: Economic Status and the Potential for Large and Family-Sized Units,* USDA Economic Research Service, Agric. Economics Report no. 216, November 1971.

[2] See figures quoted in Edwards, Angela, and Rogers, A. (eds) *Agricultural Resources,* Faber, 1964, chapter 7.

[3] OECD, *Capital and Finance in Agriculture,* 1970.

[4] Hooper, S.G. 'Ernest Sykes Memorial Lecture', *J. of Institute of Bankers,* 1967.

[5] Midland Bank (private correspondence).

[6] Wilson, J.S.G. *Availability of capital and credit to United Kingdom agriculture,* Ministry of Agriculture, Fisheries and Food, 1973.

[7] For example, if a 2½ per cent discount is lost by delaying payment by a month after it is due, the effective annual rate of the month's credit is 30 per cent. *See* Berkeley Hill, 'True costs of capital' *Farm Management,* vol. 2, no. 7, 1973/74.

[8] Britton, D.K. *Cereals in the United Kingdom: Production, Marketing and Utilisation,* Pergamon, 1969.

[9] Jackson, B.G., and Sturrock, F.G. *The National Wheat Survey: a report on a survey of the 1964 wheat crop in England and Wales,* Agricultural Economics Unit, Department of Land Economy, University of Cambridge, 1969.

[10] *Report of the Committee of Inquiry on Contract Farming,* HMSO Cmd, 5099, 1972.

[11] FAO, *Agricultural Adjustment in Developed Countries,* 1972.

[12] See note 1.

[13] Madden, J.P. *Economies of size in farming: theory, analytical procedures, and a review of selected studies,* Economic Research Service, US Dep. Agric., rep. no. 107, 1967.

[14] Indeed, if prices of products were above the lowest point of the long-run envelope average cost curve, very few firms would be operating at their lowest average cost.

[15] This is the capacity (e.g. horsepower per acre) available in one year, and is not of course a measure of the *total* services available from a machine during its remaining life; that is probably better reflected by value.

[16] Johnston, W.E. 'Economies of Size and the Spatial Distribution of Land in Farming Units', *Americal Journal of Agricultural Economics,* vol. 54, pt. 1, 1972.

[17] Data on average performances cannot reveal whether or not each business is using its variable inputs in such a way as to achieve maximum profits, that is, at peak efficiency within the constraint of its fixed resources. It can be assumed either that businesses of all sizes are operating in this way (they are said then to be in equilibrium because any re-allocation would diminish profits) or at least that non-profit maximisation bears equally on all sizes of business so that average performances are not distorted by differences in the goals of farmers. In reality, goals probably do differ marginally, but one hopes by extents too small to invalidate comparisons of size and performance.

[18] For instance for specialist dairy farms in 1971/72 the figures were:

Size-group (smd)	Gross output per acre (£)	Rent and rates per acre (£)	Gross output per £1 rent and rates (£)
275– 599	102	5·4	18·9
600–1,199	108	6·4	16·9
1,200–1,799	109	7·3	14·9
1,800–2,399	110	8·1	13·6
2,400 and over	106	7·9	13·4

Source: derived from MAFF *Farm Incomes in England and Wales 1971/72.*

[19] MAFF, *Agricultural Labour in England and Wales,* 1973.

[20] Ingham, G.K. *Size of Industrial Organisation and Worker Behaviour,* Cambridge University Press, 1970.

[21] Gasson, R. 'Turnover and size of labour force on farms', *Journal of Agricultural Economics,* vol. XXV, no. 2, 1974.

[22] The reciprocal of labour costs per £100 gross output is, of course, the gross output produced by £100 labour input (including the value of the farmer's and wife's labour), and such figures for the FMS are published in the annual report by MAFF on Farm Incomes. As expected, they show a large increase in gross output per £100 labour input between the smallest and next smallest groups of businesses, followed by a smaller increase to the next size-group, beyond which little further improvement or a slight deterioration occurs. Mixed farms are somewhat inconsistent in this respect, as the jump between the first and second size-groups is less than between the second and third. This may be 'real', or caused by the relatively small numbers of farms involved.

171

[23] Not more than 13 per cent even on the smallest size of business, except for the smallest mixed farming group, where it forms about one third.

[24] Or, less probably, unpaid family labour other than the farmer's and wife's labour.

[25] Comprising depreciation, repairs, fuel and contract services, but with no allowance for interest on the capital value of the machinery.

[26] See Food and Agriculture Organisation of the United Nations, *Agricultural Adjustment in Developed Countries,* 1972.

[27] Economic Development Committee for Agriculture, *Farm Productivity. A report on factors affecting productivity at the farm level,* 1973.

[28] Material for this section has been kindly supplied by Prof. J. de Veer, Landbouw-Economisch Instituut, The Hague.

[29] See Bauwens, A.L.G.M., Douw, L., and Schippers, J.M. *De kleine bedrijven op de zandgronden in de jaren zestig,* Landbouw-Economisch Instituut, 1971.

[30] Scott, H.G. *Factor variability and returns to scale in British agriculture,* Faculty and Commerce and Social Science, University of Birmingham, Series A, no. 102, 1969.

[31] Anderson, J.R., and Powell, R.A. 'Economies of Size in Australian Farming' *Australian Journal of Agricultural Economics* vol. 17, no. 1, 1973. *See also* Mauldon, R.G. *'Growth and economies of size on small farms',* Rm. Policy, Nedlands, W. Australia, 9.3. 1969.

[32] Buxton, B.M., and Jensen, H.R. *'Economies of size in Minnesota dairy farming',* Stu. Bull. Minn. Ag. Ex. Sta., St. Paul., Minn. 1968.

[33] Anderson, C.G., and Moore, D.S. *Economies of size on farms in the Blackland area of Texas,* Texas Experimental Station, 1972.

[34] Madden, J.P. *Economies of size in farming: theory, analytical procedures and a review of selected studies,* Economic Research Service, USDA Economic Report no. 107, 1967.

[35] Pig and poultry enterprises have frequently been the subject of specific research into economies of size, but as they are not directly land-demanding to the same extent as milk or cereals, they do not form a part of this present study of size and efficiency.

[36] Quick, A.J. *Experiences and Problems in Large-Scale Milk Production,* United Nations Economic and Social Council, Economic Commission for Europe, Committee on Agricultural Problems, 1974.

[37] Milk Marketing Board/Farm Buildings Centre, *Dairy Cow Buildings — performance and profit,* 1970.

[38] MAFF, *Costs and Efficiency in Milk Production 1968–1969,* 1972.

³⁹ Milk Marketing Board, *Costs of Milk Production in England and Wales, April 1972 to March 1973*, 1974.
⁴⁰ Comprising (in descending order of magnitude) share of farm overheads, rental value of milking buildings, dairy equipment repair and depreciation, consumable stores, veterinary services and medicines, etc.
⁴¹ An alternative to the cross-section approach is to study the effect of increases in the size of existing herds on the resulting additional labour and capital costs. The result of such a study by the MAFF is given below. The data imply that, with expansion, additional gallons require less than the existing average labour input per cow but more than the average capital input.

The results are summarised below:

Average and Marginal Labour and Capital Cost

Item	Cost per cow	
	Average	Marginal
Labour (hours)	62	45
Capital (£)	8·1	8·3
Labour + capital	29·6	27·2

Source: MAFF, *Costs and efficiency in milk production 1968–69*, 1972.

When these relationships were estimated in a linear form but with the variables expressed as logarithms the results implied that expanding herd size was subject to *increasing* marginal capital costs and *decreasing* marginal labour costs. Because the latter was more than sufficient to offset the effect of the former, the marginal cost of capital-plus-labour diminished with increasing herd size. The inference drawn from both these sets of results was that, while larger herds did use more capital, this was likely to be more than offset by economies in the use of labour, but, of course, the situation with respect to individual herds depended upon their particular circumstances.

⁴² Silvey, D.R., *Milk Production: A Comparison of England and Denmark*, Agricultural Economics Unit, Department of Land Economy, University of Cambridge, 1973.
⁴³ See note 8.
⁴⁴ Jackson, B.G., and Sturrock, F.G., *The National Wheat Survey: a report on a survey of the 1964 wheat crop in England and Wales*, Agricultural Economics Unit, Department of Land Economy, University of Cambridge, 1969.

[45] *The Economics of Oat Production in Scotland,* North of Scotland College of Agriculture, Agricultural Economics Division, School of Agriculture, Aberdeen, Economic Report no. 130, 1973.

[46] Sutherland, R.M., and Steele, R.J.G., *The Economics of Barley Production in the North of Scotland, 1968,* North of Scotland College of Agriculture, Economic Report 127, 1970.

[47] Further, though less detailed, information comes from a study of barley production in Devon and Cornwall in 1964. The direct charges to the barley crop of specialised machinery, contract charges and labour and tractor hours fell with increasing size of barley enterprise. This study concluded that the larger barley growers achieved lower total costs of production per acre, and this 'was entirely due to lower labour and power costs, although there was a wide range of results between farms with similar barley acreages'. However, because contract charges were included in labour and power costs, it is not possible to ascertain whether the major source of economies was contracting or the farms' own resources of labour and fixed capital. (*Barley production in Devon and Cornwall in 1964,* University of Exeter, Department of Agricultural Economics, Farmers Report no. 2, 1966.)

[48] 43 acres in 1960, 58 acres in 1965 and 84 acres in 1971 (England and Wales).

[49] Figures (£ per acre) were:

> 275—599   smd group (mean crops and grass acreage 155) 20·3
> 600—1,199 smd group (mean crops and grass acreage 321) 17·6
> 1,200—1,799 smd group (mean crops and grass acreage 472) 17·9
> 1,800—2,399 smd group (mean crops and grass acreage 686) 17·0
> 2,400+   smd group (mean crops and grass acreage 938) 17·6

[50] Longworth, J.W., and McLeland, W.J., 'Economies of size in wheat production' *Review of Marketing and Agricultural Economics,* vol. 40, no. 2, 1972.

[51] Vollmar, G.J., Helmers, G.A., and Retzlaff, E.J., *Wheat production costs and economies of enterprise size in growing wheat in the Nebraska Panhandle,* Nebraska Agricultural Experimental Station, Bulletin no. SB 500, 1968.

7 Conclusions

The apparent inefficiency of small farms: does it call for structural adjustment measures?

We are aware that this study cannot claim to be a thorough-going analysis of the economies of size in agriculture, since it has concentrated almost entirely on evidence of the relative levels of efficiency actually achieved at different points in the size-range, rather than on what these different sizes of farm might have been capable of achieving if the existing resources had been used to full capacity in that location. Performance which does not come near to the potentiality of the business in its given circumstances does not in itself provide evidence about economies of size. However, if, at all levels of size, the discrepancy between performance and potentiality is of about the same order of magnitude, the *apparent* economies of size such as are indicated by the data we have analysed in the foregoing chapters will not be far from the truth. Therein lies a hypothesis which has yet to be tested.

Meanwhile, the evidence of farm surveys in England and Wales strongly suggests that if efficiency is measured by output per £100 of inputs (including all family labour), then farms of less than 600–800 smd's (which corresponds on average to about 110–150 acres) are generally less efficient than farms above that size. In other words, there appears to be a kind of 'threshold' somewhere between the 2-man and 3-man size of farm business, and if that size is not attained it is likely that resources, particularly labour, are not being effectively used (Figures 5.1, 5.12 and 5.15). This situation showed little change between the mid-1950s and 1970 (Figure 5.2).

Between 25 and 30 per cent of the agricultural land in England and Wales is to be found on holdings of less than this 'threshold' size (Figures 3.3 and 3.4) although it must be noted that some 10 per cent is in part-time holdings which lie outside the scope of the main part of the present study. It is likely that many of the occupiers of the smaller farms, and especially the younger ones, are only too well aware of the handicaps imposed by the limitations of size on the effective utilisation of their resources and are constantly seeking opportunities to enlarge their businesses. This they might do either by obtaining access to more land, through purchase or renting, or by further intensifying their systems of production if this can be done without excessive use of variable inputs. In this way, they could reasonably expect to raise their efficiency and this, coupled with the increased size of business, could appreciably increase their incomes.

In acreage terms, the average size of the 2-man farm is gradually tending to increase as machinery and other equipment enables each man to manage a greater area.

For both these reasons – the economic limitations imposed by small size and the increased land-using capacity of each man – pressure is generated to create larger farm units, and the evidence of successive agricultural censuses is that small farms are steadily diminishing in number, partly by the encroachment of non-agricultural uses of land but mainly by amalgamation or 'merging' (Figures 3.7 and 3.8). The same tendency may be observed in other countries (Figures 3.9, 3.10 and 3.11). Therefore, to some extent, the low-efficiency implications of an agricultural size-structure in which there are large numbers of holdings which do not provide full employment for at least two men may be self-correcting. If present trends in England and Wales continue these holdings will, in due course, dwindle to a number far below the figure of about 50,000 which were enumerated in 1970 (Table 3.5) and will represent a relatively insignificant part of British agricultural production.

Seen in this light, it might be thought that there is not a serious problem of structural adjustment to be faced in this country. Competition between farms is sifting out the more efficient from the less efficient units and eventually the 'non-viable' units will disappear or will continue only as part-time operations with supplementary income being derived from non-agricultural sources. Strenuous efforts to raise their efficiency in their existing situation might seem to be neither necessary nor very fruitful. Our calculations indicate (p. 43) that even if the average efficiency of all the small (but full-time) farms of less than 600 smd in England and Wales could be brought up to the average level attained by larger farms, this would represent an increase of only 2 per cent in total agricultural output. Nationally, therefore, we could perhaps afford to wait for the size-structure to correct itself. This would eliminate many low-income farms and, at the same time, could be expected to bring with it a modest but useful bonus of more efficient resource use. The actual size of this bonus would depend on the extent to which the transferred resources took advantage of the economies of scale available to them in the larger unit.

The process of enlargement by amalgamation, however, is slow and often has to wait upon the cessation of an occupancy by death or retirement before it can take effect. Moreover, its merits as a largely self-generating long-term solution of 'the small farm problem' afford no consolation to the farmers who are sifted out or who are fighting a losing battle as the size constraints tighten. The solution of the social problems presented by the persistence of tens of thousands of these units is of greater importance than a mere consideration of their share in total production would suggest.

It therefore seems to us entirely right that measures should be pursued which would assist and accelerate, but not compel, the process of enlargement by the absorption of most of those farms which are of less than the 2-man size, while making proper provision for the welfare of families which are displaced as a result of these measures.

If such measures appear justifiable in England and Wales, with its relatively favourable farm size-structure, they would seem to be all the more appropriate in other countries where a far higher proportion of the farming population and the land resources is enclosed in farms of a size which cannot normally be expected to yield an acceptable standard of living in the absence of supplementary sources of income.

Future of the small farm

To support measures of structural adjustment is not to say that the small farm is doomed to extinction; that nothing can be done to improve its socio-economic status; that everything should be sacrificed to the pursuit of efficiency; or that bigger always means better. Our analysis has shown that, even among the smallest farm businesses, some can be found which can match, in terms of efficiency and even of income, many farms which greatly exceed them in size (Figures 5.13, 5.14 and 5.15 and Table 5.9). Their very existence casts doubt on the pervasiveness of economies of size. We have not been able to explore to any great depth the reasons why this should be so, though it is clear that the effective use of the farmer's own working time is often the key to the successful operation of a small business. It also seems likely that they are making use of better technology. The further investigation of the characteristics of these flourishing small farms seems well worth pursuing, especially if it could lead to the identification of the most promising ways in which the gap between them and the rest of the farms of comparable size might be reduced. In any event, it is quite clear that some small farms have a strong capacity to survive, and no categorical generalisation about the 'non-viability' of farms of below a certain size can claim any validity, even if the judgement confines itself to economic criteria and pays no regard to the other considerations which strengthen the farmers' determination to stay in business.

Considerations of economies of size must never disregard the fact that family farms are by no means always dominated by the profit-maximisation motive, still less by a desire to achieve a high efficiency ratio. Enlargement of a business brings with it increased responsibility and often a greater degree of risk and consequently of anxiety and stress than the farmer cares to contemplate. The difficulties of co-ordination and control tend to multiply. If some small farmers show no great inclination to reap the apparent benefits of larger-scale operations, this is not necessarily an irrational attitude. Similarly, if they tend to over-invest in machinery for the sake of convenience and insurance against breakdown, even when the accounts would suggest that they can ill afford to do so; or if they lavish their working hours on the care of their livestock without regard to alternative employment opportunities which have no attractions for them; can we say that the interests of efficiency should impose a different line of action?

Nevertheless, there is another argument often adduced against the case for economies of size which has little relevance to agriculture as it is practised in most farms in Britain or other Western European countries today. This is the argument that large businesses inevitably become highly impersonal, thereby depriving their employees of any sense of identity or self-respect and alienating them for their employers and from the people who ultimately consume their products. We would emphasise that the economies of size which may be of importance to British agriculture are those which are likely to occur in expanding from the one-man or two-man unit to the three-man or four-man unit. Although it must be admitted that the Farm Management Survey does not provide enough data about very large farm businesses to give any clear indications about possible economies of size at that end of the scale, we have found little evidence that any appreciable economies of size are generally to be gained by enlarging beyond the point where the farmer remains in very close contact with his employees, if indeed he has any at all outside the family. Some of the evidence seems to suggest that certain diseconomies may be experienced beyond a size of about 4,000 smd, or 15 workers (Figure 5.12).

We are impressed by the frequency with which American studies affirm that, in most farming situations, all the economies of size can be achieved by modern and fully-mechanised two-man farms, and that even one-man farms can attain highly efficient systems of operation. There seems very

178

little likelihood that 'big business', in the sense of firms employing large numbers of workers, will play a large part in British agriculture in the foreseeable future. We have shown that there is more agricultural production taking place on holdings of the two-man size (525–575 smd) than at any other size-interval of equal range (p. 30). The typical farm will remain as a family farm for a long time to come, without being excluded from the benefits of economies of size which will be available for those who choose to take advantage of them.

Index

181

182